The
Memory
Book

The
Memory
Book

How to remember anything you want

Tony Buzan™

with James Harrison, consultant editor

Harlow, England • London • New York • Boston • San Francisco • Toronto • Sydney • Singapore • Hong Kong
Tokyo • Seoul • Taipei • New Delhi • Cape Town • Madrid • Mexico City • Amsterdam • Munich • Paris • Milan

Published by BBC Active, an imprint of Educational Publishers LLP, part of the Pearson Education Group, Edinburgh Gate, Harlow, Essex, CM20 2JE, England.

First published in Great Britain in 2010

© Tony Buzan 2010

BBC Logo © BBC 1996. BBC and BBC Active are trademarks of the British Broadcasting Corporation.

ISBN: 978-1-4066-4426-5

British Library Cataloguing-in-Publication Data
A catalogue record for this book is available from the British Library

Library of Congress Cataloging-in-Publication Data
A catalog record for this book is available from the Library of Congress

Mind Map® is a registered trademark of the Buzan Organisation Limited 1990. For more information, contact: BUZAN CENTRES WORLDWIDE PLC, www.Buzancentresworldwide.com Buzan™ is a trademark of the Buzan Organisation Limited 2006.

10 9 8 7 6 5 4 3 2
13 12 11 10

Designed by Design Deluxe
Cartoon illustrations by Viv Mullett
Typeset in 9.5 Swis721 Lt BT by 30
Printed and bound in Great Britain by Ashford Colour Press Ltd, Gosport, Hants

The publisher's policy is to use paper manufactured from sustainable forests.

Dedicated to Zeus and Mnemosyne's ideal muse-child:

my dear, dear friend Lorraine Gill, the Artist

Special Consultants: Dr Sue Whiting GMM and

Grandmaster Raymond Keene, OBE

Contents

Part 4 The total learning memory technique 178

Author's acknowledgements

My heart- and mind-felt thanks to the following for their masterful and memorable performances: to Dr Sue Whiting, five times Women's World Memory Champion and first-ever female Grand Master of Memory (GMM), for her creative and unceasing efforts in helping me to refine and update SEM³, in helping others understand, appreciate and use it, and for being the current reigning 'SEM³ Champion'!; to International Chess and Mind Sports Grandmaster Raymond Keene, OBE, for his ground-breaking work on the identification and ranking of genius, and for his cogent insights into the body of Shakespeare's works; to Memory Grandmaster Ian Docherty for his ongoing help with the development of SEM³; to the wonderful artists Lorraine Gill and Christopher Hedley-Dent for their help in educating me in the appreciation of art and their intensive research support for 'the Artists' entries of this book; to my dear mother, Jean Buzan, for her 'eagle editorial eye'; to Dominic O'Brien, eight times World Memory Champion, for manifesting everything that this book says is possible.

Bringing *The Memory Book* into the twenty-first century, 'the Century of the Brain' has been a global team effort, and I would like to extend my heartfelt appreciation to the entire network of Buzan Centres International now well and truly established – and growing!

A special thank you to Jennifer Goddard at Buzan Centre Australia/NZ (and Australia's only Buzan Master Trainer) for her founding and nurturing of the Australian Memory Championships and for her support of all the World Memory Championships; thanks also to Tanya Phonanan 'the Master of Memory' in Thailand.

Thank you also to Brian Lee for being a friend and stalwart in helping me to bring the *Mind Set* series to the public; to Phil Chambers, World Mind Mapping Champion and Senior Buzan Licensed Instructor for his superb Mind Map creations and for his tireless backroom input!

My thanks also to my 'home team' at Buzan HQ including Anne Reynolds, Suzi Rockett, and Jenny Redman for their superb logistical support and effort.

At Pearson, the publishers, I would like to thank Richard Stagg, Director, who was a prime figure in the launching of this project; and to add my profound thanks to Samantha Jackson, my cherished Commissioning Editor, for her total commitment to *The Memory Book* throughout its long gestation; also to her team in Harlow, Caroline Jordan, Michelle Clark, Laura Blake. My thanks would not be complete without acknowledgement to James Harrison, my independent consultant editor for helping to shape, structure and nail everything together.

Finally my acknowledgements to all those mnemonists, Mind Mappers and memory educators who enthusiastically provided memory stories and tests, both for the first edition and this revised and updated edition, and who for reasons of space I have either omitted to thank or been unable to include.

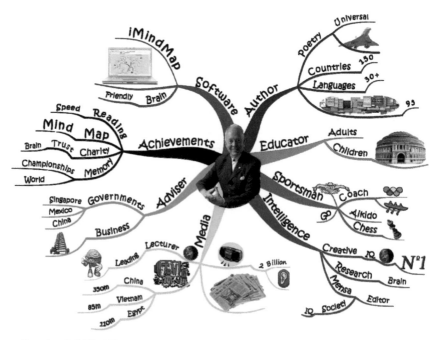

Here is a full Mind Map employing words and images and hierarchies and categorisation that radiate their own associations and increase the power of memory. It is a Mind Map about the author Tony Buzan.

Foreword

If I told you a story about a schoolboy who failed a number of his 'O' levels, left school aged 16, was told by his teachers that he would never amount to anything, but who eventually became the World Memory Champion, you would probably think I was a writer of fiction and the story could not possibly be true. However, it is true. That 'failure of a lad' was me!

After leaving school, travelling and working at various jobs, I saw a man on television called Creighton Carvello memorise a pack of cards in just under three minutes. To me this was miraculous, although it was obviously not a trick. Creighton really had memorised the cards in that staggeringly short time.

I thought, 'I have a brain the same as he has. If he can do that marvellous feat, there must be a method by which I can also do it.' I set about training myself.

After a few months, I reached the 'Holy Grail' of three minutes. Wondering what to do next with my rapidly growing 'memory muscle', I heard of the first World Memory Championships in 1991, organised by the author of the book you are now reading, Tony Buzan. I entered the competition and, after some mighty mental combat, was declared the first World Memory Champion.

The foundation principles I used to win the World Memory Champion title are those you will find outlined in this book. If you apply these principles to the matrices of knowledge that *The Memory Book* so vividly portrays, you will be able to bestride both the world of memory and the world of knowledge simultaneously, giving yourself the advantages that I found such training and application gave to me: greater self-confidence, a growing mastery of my imagination, improved creativity, vastly improved perceptual skills and, yes, a much higher IQ!

I feel honoured to be able to recommend this enlightening book, whose author has so many credentials. Besides holding the world record for creative IQ, Tony is the author and co-author of over 100 bestsellers about the brain and learning. He is also creator of the now world-famous Mind Maps and, to my mind, is one of the world's most effective communicators, both verbally and in the written word. He co-founded the Brain Trust, which gave its 2008 Brain of the Century Award to Baroness Susan Greenfield, and is Founder and President of the World Memory Sports Council, which is the governing body of the mind sport of memory and the annual World Memory Championships (held in Bahrain in 2008 and 2009). The Festival of the Mind is now in its eighteenth year and currently includes memory tests on names and faces, plus pack of cards memory – speed, multiple packs of cards – words and shapes (see the Appendix sections for more details about these and other events and organisations).

I feel privileged to have been around in those early years when I and others set modest benchmarks at the birth of a mind sport that now sees ever more countries setting up their own national memory championships and producing the memory stars of the future. As each year passes, new records are established as the standard of competition rises. How inspiring it has been to witness the performances of the greats, including Jonathan Hancock, Andi Bell, Ben Pridmore, Clemens Meyer and Gunther Karsten, as they break new ground and smash previous records.

To the cynic, the memorisation of random decimals, binary numbers and playing cards is little more than a pointless exercise. To me, it has opened up my mind and exposed the truly limitless nature of the human brain. It has given me confidence and the belief that I can learn anything if I put my mind to it, and that is very comforting and reassuring. Practising the art of memory is a beautiful thing and I thoroughly recommend it to everyone.

Congratulations on starting a journey that I know will change your life magnificently.

Dominic O'Brien

Dominic O'Brien, GMM, first and eight times
World Memory Champion

Introduction: A story you will remember for the rest of your life

Let me begin by introducing you to an event that astounded me and that gave me my first realisation that our memories could be perfect.

A student sat, frightened and enthralled. It was the first lesson of his first day at university. He, like the others in his class, had been forewarned that Professor Clark was not only the most brilliant graduate in English the university had ever had; he also looked down on his students from the height of his genius, and used his mental might to embarrass and confuse them. The Professor had deliberately come in late – to add to the tension!

Professor Clark strode nonchalantly into the room, and scanned the class with fiery eyes and a derisive smile.

Rather than going to his desk and ordering his papers in preparation, he stopped in front of his desk, clasped his hands firmly behind his back, and, with that same intent stare accompanied by a sneer, he said, 'First year English? I'll call the roll.' He then began to bark out, machine-gun fashion, the names of the petrified students:

'Abrahamson?'
'Here, sir!'

'Adams?'
'Here, sir!'

'Barlow?'
'Here, sir!'

'Bush?'

'Here, sir!'

'Buzan?'

'Here, sir!' . . .

When he came to the next name he barked out 'Cartland', to which there was a deathly silence. Looking even more intently, the Professor, like some Grand Inquisitor, made soul-burning eye contact with each petrified student, as if expecting them to 'own up' to their already-identified name. Still receiving no response, he sighed deeply, and said, at twice the speed of normal speech: 'Cartland?... Jeremy Cartland, address 2761 West Third Avenue; phone number 794 6231; date of birth September 25th 1941; mother's name Jean, father's name Gordon;... Cartland!?' Still no response! The silence became almost unbearable until, at exactly the right moment, he punctuated it with a shouted and terminal 'Absent!'

And so on and on the Professor continued, calling the roll without hesitation. Whenever a student was absent he would go through the same 'Cartland Routine', presenting the entire database about the absentee even though he could have had no way of knowing, on this first day, who was going to be present and who was going to be absent, even though he had never seen any one of the students before. To everyone in the class it became increasingly apparent that he knew, in the same astounding detail, the same basic biographical information about each of them.

When he had completed the roll call with 'Zygotski?' ... 'Here, Sir!', he looked at the students sardonically and said, with a droll smile, 'That means Cartland, Chapman, Harkstone, Hughes, Luxmore, Mears and Tovey are absent!' He paused again, and then said: 'I'll make a note of that ... some time!'

So saying, he turned and left the room in stunned silence.

To the enthralled student it was one of those moments where a life's 'Impossible Dream' became possible: the dream of training his memory so that it could, in a multitude of special situations, function perfectly.

To be able to remember the names and dates of birth and death and all the important facts about the major artists, composers, writers and other 'greats'!

To be able to remember languages!

To be able to remember the giant catalogues of data from biology and chemistry!

To be able to remember any list he wanted!

To be able to remember like the Professor!

He leapt out of his seat, charged out of the classroom and caught up with Professor Clark in the hallway. He blurted out his question: 'Sir, how did you do that?!' With the same imperious manner, the Professor responded, 'Because, son, I'm a Genius!' And once again turned away, not hearing the student's mumbled response, 'Yes, sir, I know, but still, how did you do that?!'

For two months he pestered 'The Genius', who finally befriended him, and surreptitiously in class translated for him 'the magic formula' for constructing the memory system that had allowed him to so dazzle the students on that memorable first day.

For the next 20 years the student devoured every book he could find on memory, creativity and the nature of the human brain, with the vision constantly in mind of creating new Super Memory Systems that went beyond even what his Professor had been able to accomplish.

The first of these was the Memory Mind Map, a 'Swiss army knife thinking tool for the brain', that allowed the user not only to remember with accuracy and flexibility but also to create, plan, think, learn and communicate on the basis of that memory.

After the Mind Map came the giant, enjoyable and easy-to-use Super Matrix Memory System that would act as a database, allowing people to have immediate access to whatever major information structures were important and necessary to them.

After 25 years, the New System emerged. The enthralled student was me! The one to whom I offer this New System, with delight, is you.

Let's now begin by looking at some further 'mind boggling' evidence about the capacity of our amazing brains.'

Dominic O'Brien, who contributed the Foreword to this book, can memorise 54 packs of cards shuffled together – that's 2808 cards – and make only 8 errors (4 of which he corrected himself after being told that he had made the mistakes) after staring at them once only. Most of us can't remember where we put our car keys.

Memory is both amazing and frustrating: we can see an old school photograph and recognise faces decades back, but forget what we had for breakfast that same morning! Meanwhile, the best brains in the world can crack the genetic code of life and recreate the moment just after the big bang, but the memory landscape remains largely uncharted. It is, to paraphrase Captain James T. Kirk, 'the final real frontier'.

What we do know is that our memory is phenomenal. This statement is made despite the following counter-arguments:

- most people remember fewer than 10 per cent of the names of those whom they meet

- most people forget more than 99 per cent of the phone numbers given to them

- memory is supposed to decline rapidly with age

- many people drink alcohol, and alcohol is reputed to destroy 1000 brain cells per drink

- internationally – across races, cultures, ages and education levels – there is a common experience, and fear of, having an inadequate or bad memory

- our failures in general, and especially in remembering, are attributed to the fact that we are 'only human' – a statement that implies our skills are inherently inadequate

- you will probably fail most of the memory tests in the following chapter or below.

All these, and other memory issues are addressed in this book. You will see that it is possible, with appropriate knowledge, to pass all the tests, and that names and phone numbers are easy to remember – if you know how. You will also discover that, if you use your memory, it will continue to improve throughout your lifetime and that, ultimately, your memory may not only be far better than you ever thought but it may also, in fact, be perfect.

Be positive: your memory really is perfect!

Across cultural and international boundaries, 'negative experiences' with memory can be traced not to our being 'only human' or in any way innately inadequate, but to two simple, easily changeable factors: negative mindset and lack of knowledge.

How often do you hear people in animated and enthusiastic conversation saying things like, 'You know, my memory's not nearly as good as it used to be when I was younger; I'm constantly forgetting things.' To which there is an equally enthusiastic reply, 'Yes, I know exactly what you mean; the same thing's happening to me', and off they go, arms draped around each other's shoulders, down the hill to mental oblivion. I call this the 'I've got an increasingly bad memory club'. This negative, dangerous, incorrect mindset is based on lack of proper training (which using this book will correct).

The only real difference between the middle-aged executive who has forgotten to phone someone he was supposed to and has left his mobile at the office and the seven-year-old child who realises on returning home that he's left at school his watch, his pocket money and his homework, is that the seven-year-old does not collapse into depression, clutching his head and exclaiming, 'Oh my God, I'm seven years old and my memory's going!'

Bear in mind the most often heard memory myth: that memory deteriorates as we get older. This is false. If your brain is used well and stimulated regularly, as it gets older it gets *better*. People in their eighties and nineties can be just as engaging mentally as people half their age. Brain cells don't die off with age. Good memory is not just good for learning, it's good for your quality and enjoyment of life.

Ask yourself, 'What is the number of things I actually remember each day?' Most people estimate somewhere between 100 and 10,000 items. The answer is in fact in the multiple billions. The human memory is so excellent and runs so smoothly that most people don't even realise that all the words they speak and those they listen to are instantaneously produced for consideration, recalled, recognised precisely and placed in their appropriate context. Nor do they appreciate that every moment, every perception, every thought, everything that they do throughout the entire day and throughout their lives is a function of their memories. In fact, its ongoing accuracy is almost perfect. The few odd things that we do forget are like odd specks on a gigantic ocean. Ironically, the reason we notice so dramatically the errors that we make is that they are so rare.

There are various arguments to support the theory that our memories may be perfect. Here are a few of them.

Dreams

Many of us have vivid dreams of acquaintances, friends, family and lovers we have not perhaps thought about in 20 years or more. In our dreams, however, the images are perfectly clear, all colours and details being exactly as they were in real life.

This confirms that somewhere in the brain there is a vast store of perfect images and associations that does not change with time and, with the right trigger, can be recalled. (In Chapter 18 you will learn about catching your dreams.)

Surprise random recall

Practically everyone has had the experience of turning a corner and suddenly recalling people or events from previous times. This often happens when people revisit their first school. A single smell, touch, sight or sound can bring back a flood of experiences thought to be forgotten.

This ability of any given sense to reproduce perfect memory images, the fact that the smell of bread baking or the sound of a song can bathe your mind in the past, indicates that, if there were more correct 'trigger situations', much more would and could be recollected. We know from such experiences that the brain has retained the information.

The Russian 'S' (Shereshevsky)

In the early part of this century, a young Russian journalist, Shereshevsky (in *The Mind of a Mnemonist*, by A. R. Luria, he is referred to simply as 'S'), attended an editorial meeting and, to the consternation of others there, he didn't take notes. When pressed to explain why, he became confused. To everyone's amazement, it became apparent that he really did not understand why anyone should *ever* take notes.

The explanation he gave for not taking notes himself was that he could remember what the editor said, so what was the point? On being challenged, 'S' reproduced the entire speech, word for word, sentence for sentence, and inflection for inflection.

For the next 30 years, 'S' was tested and examined by Alexander Luria, Russia's leading psychologist and expert on memory. When I met him in 1973, Luria confirmed that 'S' was in no way abnormal and his memory was indeed perfect. Luria also stated that, at a very young age, 'S' had 'stumbled upon' the 12 basic mnemonic (memory-enhancing) techniques (see page 33) and they had become part of his natural functioning.

The point is, 'S' was not unique. The history of education, medicine and psychology is dotted with similar cases of perfect memorisers. In every instance, their brains were found to be normal and, in every instance, they had, as young children, 'discovered' the basic principles of their memory's function.

Rosensweig's experiments

A Californian psychologist and neurophysiologist, Professor Mark Rosensweig spent years studying the individual brain cell and its capacity for storage. As early as 1974, he stated that, if we fed ten new items of information into any normal human brain every second for an entire lifetime, that brain would be considerably less than half full. He emphasised that memory problems have nothing to do with the capacity of our brains, but, rather, with the self-management of its apparently limitless capacity.

Penfield's experiments

In Canada, Professor Wilder Penfield discovered the capacity of human memory by mistake.

He was stimulating individual brain cells with tiny electrodes for the purpose of locating areas of the brain that were the cause of patients' epilepsy. To his amazement, he found that, when he stimulated certain individual brain cells, his patients were suddenly recalling experiences from their past. The patients emphasised that it was not simple memory, but they actually were reliving the entire experience, including smells, noises, colours, movement, tastes. These experiences ranged from a few hours before the experimental session to as much as 40 years earlier.

Penfield suggested that, hidden within each brain cell or cluster of brain cells, is a perfect store of every event of our past and, if we could find the right stimulus, we could replay the entire film.

The potential pattern-making ability of your brain

Professor Pyotr Anokhin of Moscow University, famous as Pavlov's brightest student, spent his last years investigating the potential pattern-making capabilities of the human brain. His findings were important for memory researchers.

It seems that memory is recorded in separate little patterns, or electromagnetic circuits, that are formed by our brain's interconnecting cells. Anokhin already knew that each brain contains one million million (1,000,000,000,000) brain cells, but even this gigantic number was going to be small in comparison to the number of patterns those brain cells could make among themselves.

Working with advanced electron microscopes and computers, Anokhin came up with a staggering number. He calculated that the number of patterns, or 'degrees of freedom', throughout each brain is, to use his own words:

> 'So great that writing it would take a line of figures, in normal manuscript characters, more than ten and a half million kilometres in length. With such a number of possibilities, the brain is a keyboard on which hundreds of millions of different melodies can be played.'

Your memory is the music.

Photographic memory

Also known as eidetic memory, this is a specific phenomenon of people remembering, usually for a very short time, perfectly and exactly, anything they have seen. This memory usually fades, but it can be so accurate that it enables somebody, after seeing a picture of 1000 randomly sprayed dots on a white sheet, to reproduce them perfectly.

This suggests that, in addition to the deep, long-term storage capacity, we also have a shorter-term and immediate photographic ability. It is argued that children often have this ability as a natural part of their mental functioning and we train it away by forcing them to concentrate too much on logic and language and too little on imagination and their other mental skills.

The 1000 photographs test

In one set of memory experiments, people were shown 1000 photographs, one after the other, at a pace of about a photograph per second. The psychologists then mixed another 100 photographs in with the original 1000 and asked the people to select those that they had not seen the first time through. Everyone, regardless of how they described their normal memory, was able to identify almost every photograph that they had seen previously – as well as each one they had not.

They were not necessarily able to remember the order in which the photographs had been presented, but they could definitely remember the images – an example that confirms the common human experience of being better able to remember a face than the name attached to it. This particular problem is easily dealt with by applying 'mnemonics' (see overleaf).

Mnemonics

'Mnemonics' (pronounced 'nem-on-ics') is the name given to memory aids that help you to remember something. These may be a word, a picture, a system or other device that will help you to recall a phrase, a name or a sequence of facts. The 'm' in mnemonic is silent and the word comes from the Greek word *mnemon*, which means 'mindful'.

Most of us will have used mnemonic techniques to learn things during our schooldays, even if we didn't realise it at the time. How about "i" before "e" except after "c" for grammar and spelling or the phrase '*Every Good Boy Deserves Favour*' to help remember the notes on the treble clef (from the lowest), EGBDF.

If the initial letters form a word, the mnemonic is known as an acronym (ac-ro-nim). An acronym is a word that is formed from the first letters of each word, such as UNESCO, which stands for the United Nations Educational, Scientific and Cultural Organization.

Many of us will have learned the poem 'Thirty days hath September, April, June and November . . .' to help remember which months have 30 days and which have 31 ('except for February, alone . . .'). That, too, is a mnemonic: a device to help you remember.

Mnemonics work by stimulating your imagination and using words and other tools to encourage your brain to make associations.

Experiments with mnemonic techniques have shown that, if a person scores 9 out of 10 when using such a technique, that same person will score 900 out of 1000, 9000 out of 10,000, 900,000 out of 1,000,000 and so on. Similarly, anyone who scores 10 out of 10 will score 1,000,000 out of 1,000,000.

This and other techniques and 'systems' are set out in *The Memory Book* to help you delve into that phenomenal storage capacity you have and pull out whatever it is you need. You'll be amazed at how easily they can be learned and how they can be applied in personal, family, business and community life.

A mind to memorise

Memory can be sharpened by our keenness or enthusiasm (and, equally, dulled by our disinterest or 'switching off'). The more you make of the stuff you learn, the more you will remember.

Remember, memory works by making something memorable by using the power of association and location in order to increase your facility for recall.

The World Memory Championships and Mental World Records

Since 1991, and the first memory book, *Use Your Memory*, inspired World Memory Championships, every year the limits previously placed on human memory have been shattered. In every competition, the records are continually being broken at an exponential rate. We now know, which we did not know even a few years ago, that the average human brain, if properly trained, can memorise over 2000 binary digits perfectly in an hour, can memorise over 100 names and faces in 15 minutes, can memorise a spoken number heard only once, of over 200 digits, and can memorise a deck of cards in less than 25 seconds.

All the people who set those astonishing records, have declared in public that they think they are 'only at the beginning'!

Making whatever you want to remember distinctive, relevant, and elaborating on it is what the memory contestants do at the annual World Memory Championships. These mnemonists are no cleverer than you or I; they just take the time and make the effort to memorise information using a variety of techniques and strategies – and they really remember. For instance, for years, memorising a pack of cards in under 30 seconds has been seen as the memory equivalent of beating the 4-minute mile in athletics. In the 2007 UK Memory Championships, Ben Pridmore memorised a single shuffled deck of playing cards in 26.28 seconds, beating the previous World Record of 31.16 seconds set by Andi Bell. Two years earlier, Dr Gunther Karsten from Germany memorised a 1949-digit number in an hour – and recalled it in under 2 hours (see the Appendix sections for more on the World Memory Championships).

A brief history of memory

The Ancient Greeks were the first to seek a physical, as opposed to a spiritual, basis for memory. Not surprisingly, the first person to introduce a really major idea in the field of memory was Plato, in the fourth century BC. His theory is known as the 'wax tablet hypothesis' and was accepted up until recently.

To Plato, the mind accepted impressions in the same way that wax becomes marked when a contoured object is pressed into its surface. Plato assumed that, once the impression had been made, it remained until it wore away with time, leaving a smooth surface once again. This smooth surface was, of course, what Plato considered to be equivalent to complete forgetting – the opposite aspect of the same process. As will become clear later, many people now feel that memory and forgetting are two quite different processes.

It was also the Ancient Greeks who devised the first recorded mnemonic techniques. In 477 BC, a Greek poet named Simonides of Ceos devised a memory technique called the method of 'loci', which means, literally, 'locations'. With little in the way of writing materials available, it was common for orators and others to memorise their speeches and so on by imagining a journey and then mentally tracing their steps to recall each article. The Ancient Romans continued the oral tradition and, over 2000 years later, the journey method, along with the pegging and linking memory systems detailed in this book, have become key mnemonic strategies at the annual World Memory Championships.

Modern memory research

Today, almost without exception, physiologists and other thinkers in this field agree that memory is located in the cerebrum, which is the large area of our brains covering the surface of the cortex. However, locating exactly where memory processes take place is proving a difficult task, as is achieving an accurate understanding of the function of memory itself. The current favoured sites are the hippocampus and rhinal cortex.

Another model of memory is that *every* part of the brain may include *all* memories. This model is based on how holographic photography works. In simple terms, a holographic photographic plate is simply a piece of glass, which, when two laser beams are passed through it at the right angles, reproduces a ghostly, three-dimensional photograph. One of the amazing things about this photographic plate is that, if you smash it into 100 pieces and take away any one of those 100 pieces, you can shine the two laser beams through it and still get the same (although slightly more blurred) picture. Thus, every part of the holographic photographic plate contains a mini-record of the overall picture.

The corollary is, therefore, that every one of our multimillion brain cells may, in fact, act as a mini-brain, recording, in some fantastically complex way as yet indiscernible to our clumsy measuring instruments, our entire experience.

Fantastic as this theory may sound, it goes a long way towards explaining the perfect memories we have in dreams, the surprise random recall, the memories of the perfect memorisers, the statistics from Rosensweig's experiments, as well as the mathematical grandeur of Anokhin's results, as outlined above.

Creativity and memory

The prime engine of your creativity is your *imagination*. The creative genius goes on imaginative journeys, taking people into original and previously unexplored realms. There, new *associations* give rise to the new realisations that the world calls creative breakthroughs – the works of mental genius that can shift the course of history. So it was with Leonardo da Vinci, Darwin, Archimedes, Newton, Madame Curie, Cézanne and Einstein.

The difference between memory and creativity

Thus it becomes clear that memory is the use of imagination and association to hold the past in its appropriate place and re-*create* the past in the present; whereas creativity is the use of imagination and association to plant the present thought in the future and re-*create* the present thought, whether it be a poem, symphony, scientific relationship, building or spaceship, in some future time.

The important point here is that, although the names and purposes may be slightly different, the underlying principles of *imagination* and *association* are identical. *Therefore, whenever you are practising or applying memory techniques, you are at the same time practising and enhancing your powers of creativity.*

Memory exercises

The exercises you are about to embark on in the course of this book are very much to the brain as gymnastic exercises are to the body.

The more you exercise in the 'gymnasium of mnemonics', the more the 'muscles' of your memory and creativity will be developed.

Carrying this idea a little further, a new formula for developing your genius emerges: the more *Energy* you put into developing your *Memory*, the more your *Creativity* will grow and you have an infinite capacity to do this. In other words, energy plus and 'into' memory equals infinite creativity. The formula can be written:

$$E + M = C^\infty$$

This new mental formula demonstrates that if you put energy into your memory you will produce a perfect memory, and an expanding and potentially infinite creativity. This formula also exemplifies the Greek myths: Jupiter (Energy) into Mnemosynae (Memory) yields the Muses (infinite creativity).

Modern confirmation of the Greeks' ideas

Recent brain research, especially in the area of the left and right cerebral cortex, has confirmed that all of us have, distributed throughout the most evolutionarily advanced part of our brains, an enormous range of mental skills that simply require appropriate training and development for them to manifest and grow.

Information is taken in by your brain and stored in your memory in many different ways. Also, it is processed by either the right side of your brain – concerned with rhythm, imagination, daydreaming, colour, dimension, spatial awareness, completeness – or the left – concerned with logic, words, lists, numbers, sequence, lines, analysis. These 'left and right cortical skills' are not cut off from each other, and the two sides of your brain do not operate separately from one another – indeed, they need to work together to be at their most effective. The more we can stimulate both sides of our brain at the same time, the more effectively they will work together to help us:

- think better

- remember more

- recall instantly.

The mind set skills commonly – but not exclusively – associated with the left- and right-side of our cerebral cortex: lists, words, numbers, linearity, analysis (L) ; daydreaming, colour, rhythm, dimension, and Gestalt (the whole picture) (R)

In our hind- and mid-brain, and distributed in part throughout our upper brain, exist our additional mental abilities to see, hear, smell, taste, touch, move in three-dimensional space, respond and emote.

A quick check confirms the extraordinary similarity between what the Greeks discovered by self-analysis and practice and what modern science has discovered through the elegant rigours of the scientific method.

Mesmerising memory

As I got older I became more and more fascinated by memory and committed myself to developing ways to enhance and improve my memory pathways in order to make optimum use of that amazing part of our anatomy, our brains. This led me to develop my Mind Map® technique, which is now used around the world and was also launched in computer software format as iMindMap in 2006 (see www.imindmap.com). *The Mind Map Book* tells you all about Mind Maps and how to use them to boost your memory, thinking and creativity. Even now, after working in the field for over 45 years, I am amazed at what your mind and memory can do – and how much untapped potential we each have.

It is an exciting prospect to be a part of the research into brain and memory function that is going on around the world at this very moment. The twenty-first century has been called 'The Age of Intelligence, Century of the Brain and Millennium of the Mind', and we have entered an extremely invigorating time of discovery and cerebral awakening.

Your memory and your memories are unique to you because no one else can experience life as you see it and feel it. Only you know how you experience the world and only you can choose how and when to recall past experiences. You may find that you can recall some memories as clear as crystal, whereas others seem as cloudy as muddy water or as elusive as a butterfly on the wing. By the time you have finished reading this book, though, you will be able to remember everything you wish to with stunning clarity, because you will have the tools to use your mind and memory more efficiently and powerfully than ever before.

When you were at school, were you taught anything about how your memory functions, how to use memory techniques, the nature of concentration, of thinking, motivation or creativity? For most people around the world the answer is 'no'. The memory systems described in this book are designed to work *with* your brain, not *against* it; to stimulate your senses and help your memory to store the information you choose to feed it in an ordered and easily accessible fashion. Enjoy what will be a memorable experience!

How to use this book

The Memory Book has been designed to enable you to achieve your memory goals as rapidly as possible.

It is divided into four main parts. Part 1 is a simple 'operations' manual, explaining how your brain operates and how memory works within your brain. It also has the first of many memory tests and exercises – to test how your memory is right now, before starting the book.

Part 2 introduces the core memory-boosting principles and techniques, including the linking and pegging memory systems.

Part 3 moves on to the more advanced 'major system', which can help you memorise way beyond 10 or even 100 items.

Part 4 is designed to supercharge your memory even further, using the 'self-enhancing master memory matrix' technique (SEM[3] for short), which takes you into the memory stratosphere.

In Part 1, Chapters 1 to 3 provide you with what you need to check your current memory capabilities, with background information on your memory, including the foundations and principles you will need to know to develop a superpower memory, especially the power of imagination and association. You will also learn about your memory's rhythms over time, enabling you to manage yourself and your life in such a way as to enhance increasingly your memory's functioning.

Chapters 4 to 8 lay out the essential and basic pegging, linking and other list systems for memorising ten items and more. These will not only help you remember a far greater number of items than you did before but are also great fun to learn. You will discover how to multiply any system you have learnt by first a factor of ten and then, by a factor of ten again!

Chapter 9 introduces you to the 'major system'. This system is so named because it forms the basis of a limitless series of other memory systems and can be specifically applied to the memorisation of those areas dealt with in Chapters 10 to 18, such as the memorisation of cards; the development of your IQ by using the long number memory system; telephone numbers; schedules and appointments; important historical dates, birthdays and anniversaries; and vocabulary and language learning.

Chapter 19 introduces you to the ultimate memory techniques for memorisation based on my SEM[3] technique. An additional range of topics for memorisation is introduced to expand your memory and knowledge. For those who want to take their memory skill still further, we have designed a dedicated website to help you practise and get more out of *The Memory Book*, see **www.pearson-books.com/the buzanmemorybook**.

It is recommended that you browse through the whole book first, then complete Chapters 1 to 8 to give yourself a solid foundation.

Having reached this stage, you may either continue through the book on a chapter-by-chapter basis, choosing any chapter from 9 to 18, or jump ahead to Chapter 10 and subsequently pick your preferred choices from Chapters 11 to 18. I recommend that you only tackle Chapter 19 when you are fully conversant with Chapter 9 and its applications.

Above all, make sure that, as you progress through *The Memory Book*, you use, to their fullest extent, your *associative* and *imaginative* abilities – and that you enjoy yourself!

So how good is your memory now?

Are you good at remembering some things and not others?

- How are you on facts, faces, birthdays?

- Do you believe your memory is getting worse as you get older?

- Are you worried about recalling information under pressure at work or in an exam?

- Would you like to be able to remember anything you put your mind to?

Before we continue, you need to test your memory in its current state. Chapter 1 kicks off with a series of memory tests that will give you a baseline against which you can check your progress. If you are interested in the truth about yourself and your performance now, as compared with what it will be when you have completed the book, perform these tests thoroughly. Most people do rather poorly at the beginning, improving dramatically as they progress through the chapters. Enjoy the journey – it will be memorable!

Contact Tony at tony.buzan@buzanworld.com

What **separates the average memory** from one **capable** of storing a telephone directory can be summed up in three words: **desire and technique**.

Dominic O'Brien, eight times World Memory Champion

Part 1
How memory works

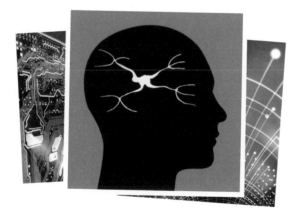

Part 1 helps you assess your current memory, explains the underlying principles of recall *during* and *after* learning and introduces you to the basic link and peg systems. These will enable you to start building up your memory banks and discover how easy it really is to boost your memory.

Checking your memory

This quick set of tests is designed to flex your memory muscles and make you aware of the false limitations we place on our memories – and, in turn, the bad habits we all fall into.

Because of the way we are trained (or not trained) in school, the exercises you will soon be attempting throughout the book may prove very difficult in some cases and in other cases almost impossible. Yet these tasks are perfectly within the capacity of the average human brain. Do not worry about a potentially poor performance, as it is the purpose of *The Memory Book* to turn poor performance into excellent performance and make memorisation an easy and enjoyable part of life.

Link test

Read the following list of 20 items through once only, trying to memorise both the items and the order in which they are listed. Then turn to page 12 to test yourself and for scoring instructions.

Wallpaper	Scissors	Power	Perfume
Mountain	Nail	Elephant	Safe
Skirt	Watch	Jail	Melon
String	Nurse	Mirror	Mongrel
Ice cream	Plant	Suitcase	Engraving

Peg test

Give yourself 60 seconds to memorise the following list of 10 items and their numbers. The aim of this test is to remember the items in random order, connecting them to their numbers. When your minute has passed, turn to page 12 and fill in the answers.

1 Atom
2 Tree
3 Stethoscope
4 Sofa
5 Alley
6 Tile
7 Windscreen
8 Honey
9 Brush
10 Toothpaste

Number test

Look at the four 15-digit numbers printed below, giving not more than half a minute of attention to each. At the end of each half minute, turn to page 13 and write down the sequence of numbers as best you can.

1 798465328185423   2 493875941254945
3 784319884385628   4 825496581198762

Telephone number test

The following is a list of ten businesses and people and their telephone numbers. Study the list for not more than two minutes and attempt to remember all the phone numbers, then turn to page 13 and answer the appropriate questions.

Name	Number
Healthfood shop	787-5953
Tennis partner	640-7336
Weather bureau	691-0262
Newsagent	242-9111
Florist	725-8397
Garage	781-3702
Theatre	869-9521
Nightclub	644-1616
Community centre	457-8910
Restaurant	354-6350

Card test

This test is designed to exercise your present capacity for remembering cards and their sequence. The list on page 8 contains all 52 cards of a normal pack in numbered order. Your task is to spend no more than five minutes looking at this list, then recall it. Turn to page 14 to fill in your answers.

1 Ten of diamonds	27 Four of hearts
2 Ace of spades	28 Two of diamonds
3 Three of hearts	29 Jack of spades
4 Jack of clubs	30 Six of spades
5 Five of clubs	31 Two of hearts
6 Five of hearts	32 Four of diamonds
7 Six of hearts	33 Three of spades
8 Eight of clubs	34 Eight of diamonds
9 Ace of clubs	35 Ace of hearts
10 Queen of clubs	36 Queen of spades
11 King of spades	37 Queen of diamonds
12 Ten of hearts	38 Six of diamonds
13 Six of clubs	39 Nine of spades
14 Three of diamonds	40 Ten of clubs
15 Four of spades	41 King of hearts
16 Four of clubs	42 Nine of hearts
17 Queen of hearts	43 Eight of spades
18 Five of spades	44 Seven of spades
19 Jack of diamonds	45 Three of clubs
20 Seven of hearts	46 Ace of diamonds
21 Nine of clubs	47 Ten of spades
22 King of diamonds	48 Eight of hearts
23 Seven of clubs	49 Seven of diamonds
24 Two of spades	50 Nine of diamonds
25 Jack of hearts	51 Two of clubs
26 King of clubs	52 Five of diamonds

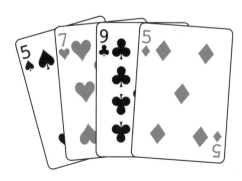

Face test

Look at these ten faces and names for not more than two minutes, then turn to pages 15–17 where the same faces are present *without* their names. Try to match the right name to the right face. Scoring instructions are on page 17.

1 Mrs Whitehead   **2** Mr Hawkins

3 Mr Fisher

4 Mr Ramm

5 Mrs Hemming

6 Mrs Briar

7 Mr Chester

8 Mr Master

9 Mrs Swanson   **10** Miss Template

Dates test

This is your last test. Listed below are ten key historical dates. Give yourself two minutes to remember them all perfectly, then turn to page 17.

then turn to page 17.

1   1666   Great Fire of London

2   1770   Beethoven's birthday

3   1215   Signing of Magna Carta

4   1917   Russian Revolution

5   1454   First printing press

6   1815   Battle of Waterloo

7   1608   Invention of the telescope

8   1905   Einstein's Theory of Relativity

9   1789   French Revolution

10   1776   American Declaration of Independence

Your responses

Link test response (see p. 5)

Note in the space provided all the items you can remember, in the correct order.

_____

_____

_____

_____

_____

_____

_____

_____

_____

_____

Score yourself in two ways: first, enter below the number of items you remembered out of 20, then record the number of items you listed in the correct order. (If you reversed two items, they are both wrong with regard to order.) Score one point for each remembered; one point for each correct placing (total possible: 40).

Number remembered: Number in correct order:

Number incorrect: Number in incorrect order:

Peg test responses (see p. 6)

In the order given below, write the items in the list next to their numbers.

10 _____   1 _____

8 _____   3 _____

6 _____   5 _____

4 _____   7 _____

2 _____   9 _____

Number correct: /10

Number test responses (see p. 6)

In the spaces below, write down each of the four 15-digit numbers.

1_____

2_____

3_____

4_____

Score one point for every digit that you record in its proper sequence.

Total score: /60

Telephone number test responses (see p. 7)

Write down, in the spaces provided, the phone numbers of the ten businesses and people.

Name	Number
Healthfood shop	_____
Tennis partner	_____
Weather bureau	_____
Newsagent	_____
Florist	_____
Garage	_____
Theatre	_____
Nightclub	_____
Community centre	_____
Restaurant	_____

Score one point for each correct number (even if you make only one mistake in the number you must consider if totally wrong, for if you had dialled it you would not have got through to the intended person or business). The highest possible score is 10.
Score: /10

Card test response (see p. 7)

(see p. 7)

Recall the list in reverse order (52–1), as indicated.

52	_____	26	_____
51	_____	25	_____
50	_____	24	_____
49	_____	23	_____
48	_____	22	_____
47	_____	21	_____
46	_____	20	_____
45	_____	19	_____
44	_____	18	_____
43	_____	17	_____
42	_____	16	_____
41	_____	15	_____
40	_____	14	_____
39	_____	13	_____
38	_____	12	_____
37	_____	11	_____
36	_____	10	_____
35	_____	9	_____
34	_____	8	_____
33	_____	7	_____
32	_____	6	_____

The Memory Book

31	_____	5	_____
30	_____	4	_____
29	_____	3	_____
28	_____	2	_____
27	_____	1	_____

Score one point for each correct answer.

Score: /52

Face test responses (see pp. 9–11)

Fit the names to the faces.

8 _____

7 _____   6 _____

1 _____

5 _____

3 _____

2 _____

9 _____

4 _____   10 _____

Score one point for each correct answer.
Score: /10

Dates test response (see p. 11)

(see p. 11)

9 _____   French Revolution

6 _____   Battle of Waterloo

1 _____   Great Fire of London

10 _____   American Declaration of
                         Independence

2 _____   Beethoven's birthday

5 _____   First printing press

4 _____   Russian Revolution

3 _____   Signing of Magna Carta

8 _____   Einstein's Theory of Relativity

7 _____   Invention of the telescope

Score one point for an accurate answer and half a point if you
come within five years. Ten is a perfect score.

Score: /10

Your scores

Now, below, enter your scores and calculate your total score for all the tests – perfect is 192.

Test result summary

Test	Your score	Possible total
Link test		40
Peg test		10
Number test		60
Telephone number test		10
Card test		52
Face test		10
Dates test		10
Total		192

To calculate your Summary Percentage Score, divide your raw score (YS) into the possible total (PT) $\left(\frac{PT}{YS} = X\right)$. Next divide the result (X) into 100 $\left(\frac{100}{X}\right)$.

= Your Summary Percentage Score

This completes your initial testing (there will be other tests for you to experiment with throughout the book).

Normal scores for each of these tests range from 20 to 60 per cent. Even a score of 60 per cent, which in the average group is considered excellent, is well below what you can expect of yourself when you have absorbed the information in this book. The average trained memoriser scores between 95 and 100 per cent for each of the tests.

The next chapter outlines two fundamental principles of memory that you should grasp before you learn the core systems of memory learning set out in the later chapters.

Your memory's rhythms

There are two major areas of memory that, if you understand them, will enable you to double the efficiency of your memory. The first happens while you are taking in information and is known as 'recall *during* learning'. The second occurs after you have taken in the information and so is called 'recall *after* learning'.

Recall during a learning period

In order for you to see clearly how your memory rhythms function during a standard learning period, it will be useful for you to experience a brief 'recall during a learning period' yourself. To do this, follow these instructions carefully: read the following list of words, one word at a time, once only, without using any memory systems or techniques and without going back over any words. The purpose of your reading the list will be to see how many of the words you can remember without using any memory principles. Simply try to remember as many of the words in order as you can.

Start reading down the columns of words now.

was	the	range
away	of	of
left	beyond	and
two	Leonardo da Vinci	and
his	which	else
and	the	the
the	must	walk
far	and	room
of	of	drawing
and	could	small
that	the	change

Once you have completed reading the list, cover it up and write down as many of the 33 words as possible below.

_____

_____

_____

_____

_____

_____

_____

_____

_____

_____

_____

_____

_____

_____

_____

_____

_____

_____

_____

Check your recall

Now check the way in which your own memory worked.

- How many words from the beginning of the list did you remember?

- How many words from the end of the list did you remember?

- Did you recall any words that appeared more than once?

- Were there any words in the list that stood out in your memory as very different?

- How many words from the middle of the list did you remember (that you have not already noted)?

In this test almost everyone recalls the information similarly:

- one to seven words from the beginning of the list

- one or two words from the end of the list

- most of the words that appear more than once (in this case, the, 'and', and 'of')

- the outstanding word or phrase (in this case, Leonardo da Vinci)

- relatively few, if any, words from the middle of the list.

Why should these similarities occur? This pattern of results shows that memory and understanding do not work in the same way: although all the words were understood, not all of them were remembered.

Our ability to recall information we understand is related to several factors.

- We tend to remember *first things* and *last things* more easily than *things in between*. Therefore we recall more information from the beginning and the end of a learning period.

- We learn more when things are associated or linked in some way, by using rhyme, repetition or something that connects with our senses. In the case of the word recall test you have just done, repetitive words include 'the', 'and' and 'of', while the associated words include 'Leonardo Da Vinci' and 'drawing'.

- We also learn more when things are outstanding or unique. In the word recall test, the outstanding item is Leonardo Da Vinci.

Taking breaks is important

Short, carefully spaced breaks are an important part of the learning and memory process. We find it easier to recall information accurately when learning if we take breaks briefly and regularly. That is because breaks allow your mind time to absorb what has been learned.

The graph on page 23 shows three different patterns of recall over a two-hour period of learning. The top line shows the pattern when four short breaks have been included. The raised peaks show the moments when recall is highest. There are more high points on this line than any of the other memory curves because there are four 'beginnings and endings'. Recall remains high.

The middle line shows a recall curve when no break has been taken. The beginning and end points show the highest level of recall, but, overall, the retention drops to well below 75 per cent.

The bottom line shows what happens if no break is taken for the period of two hours. This approach is obviously counter-productive as the recall line falls steadily downwards, to below the 50 per cent mark.

So, the more well-spaced, short breaks we have when we are learning and the more beginnings and endings we have, the better our brain will be able to remember. Brief breaks are also essential for relaxation: they relieve the muscular and mental tension that inevitably builds up during periods of intense concentration.

The rhythms of remembering

Relating all of this to yourself and to time, ask yourself the following question. If you had been studying a difficult text for 40 minutes, had found your understanding was fairly poor throughout and had noticed that, during the last ten minutes of your reading, your understanding had begun to improve slightly, would you:

(a) stop studying immediately and conclude that, as you had started to do well, you could now stop and have a rest; or

(b) carry on, assuming that now your understanding was flowing more smoothly, you'd be able to keep it going until it trailed off, then take your break?

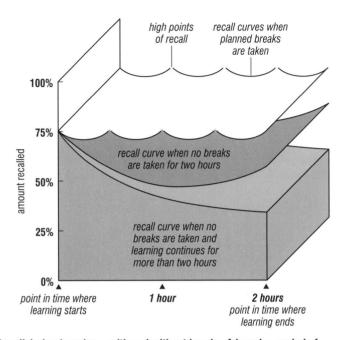

Recall during *learning – with and without breaks. A learning period of between 20–50 minutes produces the best relationship between understanding and recall*

Most people assume that, if their understanding is going well, all other things will also be going well. It can, however, be seen from the results of the test you have just taken, and from your own personal experience, that understanding and recall are not the same. They vary in amounts enormously and the factor that defines their difference is your self-management in time.

What you understand you do not necessarily recall and, as time progresses, while you learn, you will recall less and less of what you are understanding if you do not in some way solve the problem of the large dip in recall that occurs during the middle of the learning period (see graph). This 'memory rhythm' applies no matter what you are learning, and that includes the learning of memory systems.

What you are looking for is a learning situation in which both *recall* and *understanding* can work in maximum harmony. You can create this situation only by organising the time in which you are learning in such a way as to enable your understanding to remain high without giving your memory a chance to sag too deeply in the middle.

Slicing your time

This is easily accomplished by learning to divide your learning periods into the most beneficial time units. These units, on the average, turn out to be between 10 and 50 minutes after the starting point – 30 minutes for example. A shorter period does not give your mind long enough to assimilate what is being learned. This will make sense to all of us. Whether studying, in a lesson or a meeting, on the telephone or in concentrated conversation, an ideal is to maintain full attention and interest for longer than 20 to 50 minutes.

If your time is organised in this way, several advantages immediately become apparent.

- Each of the inevitable dips in your memory during learning will not be as deep as if you had carried on without the break.

- Instead of only two high points of recall at the beginning and end of the learning period, you will have as many as eight 'beginning and ending' high points of recall.

- Because you are taking breaks, you will be far more rested during your next learning period than you would have been had you continued to work without breaks. The additional advantage of this is that, when you are rested, both recall and understanding function more easily and efficiently.

- Because when you are taking breaks you are both more rested and recalling more of each learning session, your comprehension of the next new section in which you find yourself after the break will be greater because you will have laid a firmer foundation from which you can then nourish and associate the new information. The person who has not taken such breaks, in addition to a growing fatigue, will be recalling less of what he has learned before and therefore will be able to make continually fewer and fewer connections between the dwindling amount of information he has learned and the increasingly formidable and non-understandable information that threatens him.

Your breaks should usually be no longer than two to ten minutes. During each break you can allow your mind to rest by going for a short walk, making yourself a light non-alcoholic drink, doing some form of physical exercise, auto-suggesting, meditating, or listening to quiet music.

To consolidate and improve your memory even further, it is advisable at the beginning and end of each learning period to perform a very quick review of what you have learned in the previous learning periods and preview of what you are going to learn in the coming ones. This continuing review–preview cycle helps to further consolidate the information you already have, gives you growing confidence and success as you progress, allows your mind to direct itself towards the next learning target and gives you a bird's-eye view of the territory you are going to explore mentally during your entire learning session.

Understanding the rhythms of your memory in time during a learning period and using your creative imagination will enable you to form imaginative links and associations throughout your period of study, consequently transforming the sags in the middle of learning periods into nearly straight lines.

Once you have read the next chapters on memory systems, you will develop other ideas of how to link associations to remember this sequence.

Recall after learning

Once you have made it easier for your recall to work well *during* a learning period, it is important for you to do the same thing for your recall *after* the learning period. The pattern of recall after learning contains two 'surprises':

- you retain more of what you have learned *after* a few minutes have passed since the end of your learning period

- you lose 80 per cent of the detail you have learned within 24 hours of having learned it (techniques designed to help you 'take the coats off' your 'memory coat hangers' are covered in the next chapters).

The rise is beneficial, so you want to make use of it, but the decline can be disastrous, so you usually need to make sure that it does not happen. The method for both maintaining the rise and preventing the decline is 'review with repetition'.

Review with repetition

New information is stored first in your short-term memory. To transfer information to your long-term memory takes rehearsal and practice. On average, you will need to repeat an action at least five times before the information is transferred permanently to your long-term memory. That means you need to revisit what you have learned, using one or more of the memory techniques, on a regular basis. This neatly condenses into your first memory formula:

STM ® LTM = 5R

This formula translates into: 'from Short Term Memory into Long Term Memory requires Five Repetitions/Reviews/Recalls.'

My recommendations are to review and repeat what you have learned:

- shortly after you have learned it
- one day after you have learned it
- one week after you first learned it
- one month after you first learned it
- three to six months after you first learned it.

With each period of recall, you are revisiting the information that you have learned and you are also adding to your knowledge. Your creative imagination has a part to play in long-term memory and the more you go over information you have learned, the more you will link it to other information and knowledge that you already retain.

Therefore contrary to 'common sense', your memory of what you have learned rises during the breaks you take rather than immediately beginning to fall. This rise is due to the fact that your left and right hemispheres 'sort things out' for a little while on an unconscious level after you have finished taking in information during a learning period. When you return to your learning after the break, you are therefore actually in possession of more conscious knowledge than if you had carried on without the break. This last piece of information is particularly important because it dispels those deep feelings of guilt that you may experience when you find yourself naturally taking a break but at the same time thinking that you ought to be getting 'back to the grindstone'.

Why review?

If you have been studying for one hour, the high point in your recall after learning will occur approximately ten minutes *after* you stop. This high point is the ideal time for your first review. The function of the review is to imprint the information you already have in your mind, in order to make it more 'solid'.

If you manage to review at the first high point, the graph of recall after learning changes. Instead of the detailed information being lost, it is maintained. So, if you study for an hour, your first review should take place 10 minutes after you stop and your second review 24 hours later. From then on, your reviews should take place at the intervals indicated on the graph overleaf. On average, these intervals are based on units of time you find on a calendar, such as days, weeks, months, years. Thus, you would review after one day, then after one week, then after one month, then after half a year.

Each review need not take very much time. The first one should consist of reviewing and mind mapping your notes on the information you're trying to learn after the learning period. This may take as much as ten minutes for a one-hour learning period.

After the first review, each subsequent review should consist of a quick jotting down, in Mind Map form, of the basic information in your area of interest, then a comparison of your quick notes with your basic notes. Any areas you have missed out can be filled in and any new knowledge you may have acquired during the period between reviews can be added to your marginal notes.

In this manner, your recall of all the information that you need to have constantly available can be guaranteed.

It is useful to compare the minds of people who consistently review with the minds of those who do not. People who do not review are continually putting information in and letting that same information drain out. These people will find it difficult to take in new information because the background knowledge they need to understand that new information will have gone. In such cases, learning will be difficult,

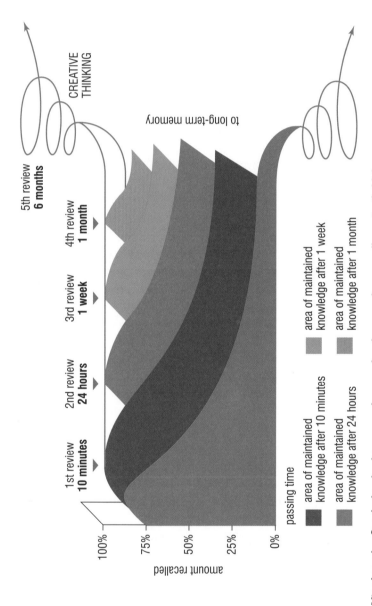

Recall After Learning Graph showing how properly spaced reviews can keep recall constantly high

1st review **10 minutes**

2nd review **24 hours**

3rd review **1 week**

4th review **1 month**

5th review **6 months**

CREATIVE THINKING

to long-term memory

passing time

amount recalled

100%

75%

50%

25%

0%

area of maintained knowledge after 10 minutes

area of maintained knowledge after 24 hours

area of maintained knowledge after 1 week

area of maintained knowledge after 1 month

recall will always be inadequate and the whole process of learning, understanding and recall will be unpleasant and arduous. People who do review will find that, with the constantly available store of increasing information, new information will slot in more easily. This will create a positive cycle in which learning, understanding and recall assist one another, making the continuing process increasingly easy.

Age-proof your memory

This information on recall after learning can also be applied to our current attitudes towards the decline of mental abilities, especially memory, with age. Most of our current statistics indicate that, as human beings grow older, our memories increasingly worsen after the age of 24. These findings, substantial as they seem, contain a major fault. They are based on surveys that studied people who generally did not have any information about how their memories worked and who consequently tended to neglect them. In other words, the tests showing that human memory declines with age were performed on people who consistently did not use any memory techniques and did not review what they had learned.

Recent experiments on people who *have* applied memory techniques and properly managed their memory rhythms during and after learning have shown that the opposite of the established findings is, in fact, the case. If you continue to use the numerical, linguistic, analytical, logical and sequential abilities of the left side of your brain, and if you continue to use the rhythmical, musical, imaginative, colourful and dimensional abilities of the right side of your brain, along with the memory time rhythms (and the memory principles you will learn in the following chapters) – all with a continual self-educating approach – your memory will *not* decline with age. Instead, it will actually improve enormously. The more it is fed, the more it will enable you to build up imaginative and associative networks with new areas of knowledge and, thus, the more it will be able to both remember and create.

Next we will look at the fundamental principles and systems for supercharging your memory. Remember: the more you give your memory, the more your memory will give back to you, and with compound interest.

The imagination and association principles and the 12 memory techniques

The Greeks worshipped memory so much, they even had a memory goddess – Mnemosyne. The word 'mnemonics' comes from her name and refers to the memory techniques that you will learn in this chapter.

In Greek and Roman times, senators would learn mnemonic techniques in order to impress other politicians and the public with their phenomenal powers of learning and memory. Using these simple but sophisticated methods, the Romans were able to remember, without fault, thousands of items, including statistics relating to their empire, and became the rulers of their time. Long before we had discovered the intricate structures of the brain and the functions of the left and right hemispheres, the Greeks had intuitively realised there are two underlying principles that ensure perfect memory: imagination and association.

Use your imagination and link in to association

Whereas, in current times, most of us are actively discouraged from using our imaginative abilities and, consequently, learn very little about the nature of mental association, the Greeks emphasised these two foundation stones of mental functioning and opened the way for us to develop the techniques even further.

Quite simply, if you want to remember anything, all you have to do is to associate (link) it with some known or fixed item (the memory systems in this book will give you those easily remembered fixed items), calling on your imagination throughout.

The more you stimulate and use your imagination, the more you will enhance your ability to learn. That is because your imagination has no limits; it is boundless and it stimulates your senses and, therefore, your brain. Having an unlimited imagination makes you more open to new experiences and less inclined to hold yourself back from learning new things.

The most effective way to remember something is to think about it as an image, in association with something else that is already fixed and known to you. If you ground your images in reality by associating them with something that is familiar, it will anchor them in a location and you will be able to remember the information more easily.

Association works by linking or pegging information to other information. For example, if you think about a banana, you will associate it with the colour yellow, its country of origin, its shape, taste, where you might buy it and store it. You will have an image of the banana and a location for it. Association works in partnership with your imagination.

Imagination and association are at the heart of all the techniques in this book – they are the foundation stones on which memory techniques are based. The more effectively you can use them, through key memory devices such as words, numbers and images, the more supercharged and effective your mind and memory will be.

As explained in Chapter 2, for your brain to work effectively you need to engage both hemispheres – the left and right sides. It can be no coincidence that the two foundation stones of memory coincide with the two main activities of the brain: imagination + association = memory.

Your memory gives you your sense of who you are, so it is appropriate that the mnemonic to remember this is 'I am'.

Imagination and association are supported by the core memory techniques that are explained below and used in Part 2 and its chapters. These help to anchor events in your memory and make it easier to recall them on demand. In addition to associating with something familiar, to remember something effectively your memory needs to have: a wonderful, multicoloured, multisensory image that stimulates your imagination, your senses and brings your memory alive.

The third memory principle

In addition to association and imagination, the Ancient Greeks added a third 'pillar of memory', which was *location*.

In other words, for your brain to remember something that it has imagined and associated, it must also have located that memory/image in a special place (this is described fully in Chapter 7).

The 12 memory techniques

- Senses
- Movement
- Association
- Sexuality
- Humour
- Imagination
- Number

- Symbolism
- Colour
- Order and/or sequence
- Positive images
- Exaggeration

As we have seen, the principles for perfect memory laid down by the Greeks fit in exactly with the information we now know about the left and right hemispheres of our brains. Without such scientific knowledge, the Greeks realised that, in order to remember well, you

A Mind Map showing the memory techniques and system outlined in this chapter

have to use every aspect of your mind, as will be outlined in this chapter. You must also include in your associated and linked mental landscape the following 12 memory techniques (see bullet list on page 33), which can be remembered by means of a mnemonic of their initial letters – SMASHIN' SCOPE.

Senses

Most of the great 'natural' memorisers and all of the great mnemonists developed an increased sensitivity to each of their senses, then blended these senses to produce enhanced recall. The blending of the senses is known as synaesthesia. In developing the memory it was found to be essential to sensitise increasingly and train your senses of vision, hearing, smell, taste, touch and kinaesthesia (your awareness of bodily position and movement in space) regularly.

Movement

In any mnemonic image, movement adds another giant range of possibilities for your brain to 'link in' and, thus, remember. As your images move, make them three-dimensional. As a subdivision of movement, use rhythm in your memory images. The more rhythm and variation of rhythm in your mental pictures, the more they will be outstanding and, thus, the more you will remember them.

Association

This is one of the two building blocks of memory, as described above. Whatever you wish to memorise, make sure you associate or link it to something stable in your mental environment. This is the peg system – number 1 = paintbrush (see page 61), for example. See also the link system (page 45).

Sexuality

We all have a good memory in this area. Use it!

Humour

The funnier, more ridiculous, absurd and surreal you make your images, the more outstandingly memorable they will be. Have fun with your memory.

Imagination

As already noted, this is also the powerhouse of your memory. Einstein said, 'Imagination is more important than knowledge. For knowledge is limited, whereas imagination embraces the entire world, stimulating progress, giving birth to evolution' ('What life means to Einstein: an interview by George Sylvester Viereck', *Saturday Evening Post*, 26 October 1929). The more you apply your vivid imagination to memory, the better your memory will be.

Number

Numbering adds specificity and efficiency to the principle of order and sequence.

Symbolism

Substituting a more meaningful image for a normal, boring or abstract concept increases the probability that you will recall it. Alternatively, you can use traditional symbols, such as a stop sign or light bulb.

Colour

Whenever possible, use the full rainbow (ideally vibrant/highlighter shades) to make your ideas more 'colourful' and, therefore, more memorable (see example opposite).

Order and/or sequence

In combination with the other principles, order and/or sequence gives you immediate reference points and so increases your brain's possibilities for 'random access'. Examples are little to big, colour grouping, sorting by category and hierarchical aggregation.

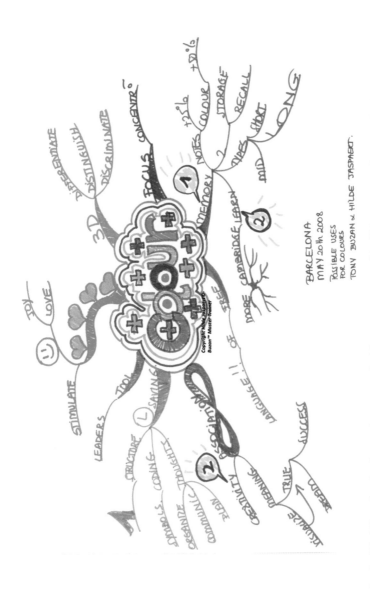

An example of a Mind Map showing how colour can make ideas more memorable. This was part of a group brainstorming session facilitated by Tony Buzan and created by Master Buzan Trainer Hilde Jaspaert

Positive images

In most instances, positive and pleasant images were found to be better for memory purposes, because they made the brain want to return to the images. Even when all the principles above were applied and though, they were 'memorable', certain negative images, could be blocked by the brain because it found the prospect of returning to such images unpleasant.

Exaggeration

In all your images, exaggerate size (large and small), shape and sound and, therefore, increase their memorability.

It is interesting to note that the principles laid out in SMASHIN' SCOPE also form the core structure of Mind Maps, and it was my exploration of memory principles that led me to develop the Mind Map initially as a mnemonic device (see *The Mind Map Book* to learn all about Mind Maps).

Key memory image words

In each memory system there is a key word. This word is the 'key memory word', in that it is the constant peg on which you will hang the other items you wish to remember. This key memory word is specifically designed to be an 'image word' – it must produce a picture or image in the mind of the person using the memory system, hence the phrase 'key memory image word'.

Purity

As you progress through the increasingly sophisticated mnemonic systems outlined in the following chapters, you will realise the importance of being sure that the pictures you build in your mind contain *only* the items you want to remember. Also, those items or words must be associated with or connected to your key memory images.

The connections between your basic memory system images and the things you wish to remember should be as fundamental, pure and uncomplicated as possible. This may be accomplished as follows:

- crashing things together
- sticking things together
- placing things on top of each other
- placing things underneath each other
- placing things inside each other
- substituting things for each other
- placing things in new situations
- weaving things together
- wrapping things together
- having things talk
- having things dance
- having things share their colour, aroma, action.

By now it will be clear to you that the systems worked out by the Greeks, and for nearly 2000 years discarded as mere tricks, were, in fact, based on the ways in which our brains actually function. The ancients realised the importance of words, order, sequence and number – now known to be functions of the left side of the cortex – and imagination, colour, rhythm, dimension and daydreaming – now known to be right-cortex functions.

Mnemosyne was, to the Greeks, the most beautiful of all the goddesses – proved by the fact that Zeus spent more time in her chamber than in those of any of the other goddesses or mortals. He slept with her for nine days and nights, and the result of that coupling was the birth of the nine Muses – the goddesses who pre-side over love poetry, epic poetry, hymns, dance, comedy, tragedy, music, history and astronomy.

For the Greeks, then, the infusion of energy (Zeus) into memory (Mnemosyne) produced both creativity and knowledge. They were correct. This is reflected in the new mental formula for developing your genius, outlined on page xxvi. If you apply the mnemonic principles and techniques appropriately, your memory will improve in the areas outlined in this book but also your creativity will soar. With these twin improvements, your overall mental functioning and assimilation of knowledge will accelerate at the same fantastic pace.

The following chapters take you from the very simple systems through to the more advanced ones, and the SEM^3 system, which will enable you to remember tens of thousands of items.

As a child I had a **conventionally good memory**. But once you learn a technique like the **location technique** it takes everything beyond what you can do **naturally**.

Former World Memory Champion Andi Bell, who can recall 10 shuffled packs of playing cards placed in front of him with just 20 minutes to memorise the order of every single card – that's 520 cards

Part 2

The core systems of memory training

Part 2 looks at the classic how-to-boost-your-memory techniques – including the link, peg and number-shape and number-rhyme systems – that are guaranteed to help your memory improve. By improving your memory, your imaginative powers and your creativity will also be released.

The link system

The most basic of all the memory systems, the link system gives you a foundation that makes learning the most advanced systems extremely easy.

This basic system is used for memorising short lists of items, such as for shopping, and each item is linked to, or associated with, the next. While using this system, you will be employing all of the 12 memory techniques described for the acronym SMASHIN' SCOPE (see page 33). By using all the principles and skills described in Chapter 3, you will be exercising the dynamic relationship between your left and right hemispheres and your senses, thereby increasing the overall power of your brain.

An example

Imagine that you have been asked to shop for the following items:

1   a silver serving spoon
2   six drinking glasses
3   bananas
4   pure soap
5   eggs
6   biological washing powder
7   dental floss
8   wholemeal bread
9   tomatoes
10   roses

The link system: Illustrating how items are linked in an exaggerated way. The sequence involves memory triggers to stimulate all your senses – imagination, exaggeration, absurdity, association, colour...

Instead of scrambling around for a bit of paper when you get there or trying to remember all the items by simply repeating them and, consequently, forgetting at least two or three, simply apply the 12 memory techniques as follows.

1 Imagine yourself walking out of your front door perfecting the most amazing balancing trick. In your mouth is the most enormous silver-coloured *serving spoon*, the handle-end of which you are holding between your teeth. Taste and feel the metal in your mouth.

2 Carefully balanced in the bowl-end of the spoon are six exaggeratedly beautiful crystal *drinking glasses*, through which the sunlight sparkles brilliantly into your bedazzled eyes. As you look with delighted amazement at the glasses, you can also hear them deliberately tinkling on the silver spoon.

3 As you make your way on to the street, you step on the most gigantic yellow- and brown-coloured *banana*, which skids with a swish from under you.

4 Being a fantastic balancer, you just about manage to not fall and confidently place your other foot on the ground, only to find that you have stepped on a shimmering white bar of *pure soap*.

5 This being too much for even you to master, you fall backwards and land, seat down, on a mound of *eggs*. As you sink into them, you can hear the cracking of the shells, see the yellow of the yolks and the white of the albumen and feel the dampness soaking into your clothes.

6 Using your imaginative ability to exaggerate, speed up time and imagine that, in a couple of seconds, you have gone back inside, undressed, and washed your soiled clothes in a super *biological washing powder*, called pure soap, which allows pure, shimmering water to leave the washing machine, and then visualise yourself once again on your way out of the front door.

7 This time, because you are slightly tired by the previous accident, you are pulling yourself along towards the shops on a gigantic rope made of millions of strands of *dental floss*. The rope connects your front door to the chemist's shop.

8 Just as all this exertion begins to make you feel hungry, wafting on the warm wind comes an incredibly strong aroma of freshly baked *wholemeal bread*. Imagine yourself being dragged by the nose as you salivate extraordinarily, thinking of the taste of the freshly baked bread.

9 As you enter the baker's shop, you notice to your amazement that every loaf on the baker's shelves is filled with brilliantly pulsating red *tomatoes* – the baker's latest idea for a new flavour.

10 As you walk out of the baker's shop, noisily munching on your tomato and wholemeal loaf, you see walking down the road with the most amazing rhythm the sexiest person you have ever seen (really let your imagination go on this one). Your immediate instinct is to buy the person *roses*, so you dive into the nearest flower shop, which sells nothing but red roses, and buy the lot, bedazzled by the redness of the flowers, the feel of the flowers as you carry them and the fragrance from the roses themselves.

It is a 'silly' story and the stuff of children's tales or wild dreams, but by this method each familiar item is linked, in an exaggerated way, to the next. The sequence involves and stimulates all your senses, with memory triggers embedded within the sequence. The triggers are movement, sequence, colour, attraction, humour, exaggeration and order.

These are all designed to encourage imagination and associa-tion and engage your memory. When you have finished reading this fantasy, close your eyes and run back through the image-story you have just read.

If you think you can already remember all ten items in the shop-ping list, turn now to the next page and fill in the answers. If not, read through this chapter again, carefully visualising on your mind's inner screen, in sequence, the events of the story.

Look at the next page when you are ready.

Record your list

Note below the ten items you had to buy.

1 _____

2 _____

3 _____

4 _____

5 _____

6 _____

7 _____

8 _____

9 _____

10 _____

If you scored 7 or more, you are already in the top 10 per cent of scores for the memorisation of such a list. You have now used the basic keys for unlocking much of the limitless potential of your brain. Now let's try memorising a list linked to knowledge and learning.

Superlinking the planets of our solar system

The memory test you are about to take concerns the planets of the solar system. It is duly noted that one planet has been 'downgraded' from full planetary status to its new status as a 'dwarf planet'. It still remains in the general category of a 'planet', so, for the purposes of this memorisation exercise, we have left it in. Having researched this area for the last 25 years, I have found that, in the average audience of 1000 people, the following statistics apply:

- 990 out of 1000 have learnt and at some time memorised the planets

- in each individual's lifetime, they have been 'exposed' to this information, either at school or through various media, for a total number of hours ranging between 5 and 100

- 100 out of 1000 *think* that they know how many planets there are in the solar system

- 40 out of 1000 *know* that they know how many there are.

- 10 think that they know the order of the planets, from the sun to the farthest planet

- 10 out of 1000 would be willing to bet on it!

The reason for this staggering loss of knowledge lies in the fact that we are never taught *how* to remember.

Check your knowledge and experience with this particular memory task and circle 'yes' or 'no':

- Did you learn the planets of the solar system and, if so, how many times and over what period of time? Yes/No

- Do you know the currently accepted number of planets in the solar system? Yes/No

- Do you know their names? Yes/No

- Do you know the normal order of the planets in the solar system? Yes/No

The solar system test

Write down the names of all the planets of our solar system. Referring to the illustration below, with the Sun in the bottom left-hand corner, put the planet names where you think they should go next to the numbers 1–9. (Just to give you a clue, Aquarius is not a planet!)

When completed, see the following pages for the correct planet order. Give yourself one mark for each planet correctly placed. If you have the correct planet name but in the wrong place, you score 0, in the same way you would if you mixed up the digits of a telephone number!

The average score around the world on this test is between one and two, so don't worry if yours is a low score.

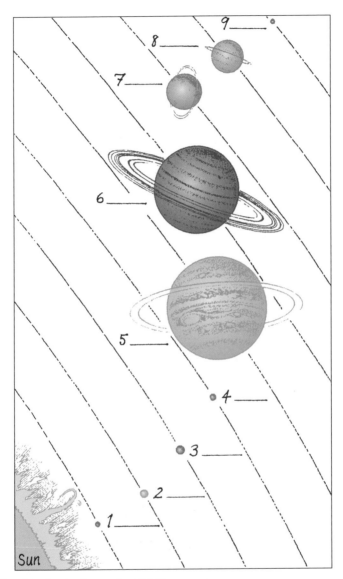

The nine planets of our solar system

Memorising the planets of our solar system

The following exercise will change the way you use your memory for ever, increase your memory power and enable you to complete a memory task that most people never accomplish in a lifetime!

Follow the instructions carefully, let your imagination run free and prepare to be amazed.

As mentioned below, for the purposes of this exercise there are nine known planets in the solar system.

In order from the Sun, they are:

1 Mercury (small)

2 Venus (small)

3 Earth (small)

4 Mars (small)

5 Jupiter (giant)

6 Saturn (giant)

7 Uranus (giant)

8 Neptune (giant)

9 Pluto (small)

In order to memorise the planets for life, you are going to use a link system in conjunction with your imagination to create a linked and fantastic story. If you follow it carefully and completely, it will be harder for you to forget it than it is for you to remember!

Imagine that, in front of you, where you are currently reading, is a glorious SUN. See it clearly, feel its heat and admire its orangey red glow.

Imagine, next to the Sun, a little (it's a little planet) thermometer, filled with liquid metal used to measure temperature: MERCURY.

Imagine that the Sun heats up and eventually becomes so hot that it bursts the thermometer. You see in front of you, tiny balls of that liquid metal, mercury.

Next, imagine that, rushing in to see what happens and then standing by your side, comes the most beautiful little goddess. Colour her, clothe her (optional!), perfume her, design her as you will. What shall we call our little goddess? Yes, VENUS!

You focus so intently on Venus with all your senses that she becomes almost a living physical reality in front of you. You see Venus play like a child with the scattered mercury and finally manage to pick up one of the mercury globules.

She is so delighted that she throws it in a giant arc, way up in the sky (which you see, as light glistens off it throughout its journey), until it hurtles down from on high and lands in your garden with a gigantic thump, which you both hear and feel as a bodily vibration.

On what planet is your garden? EARTH, of course.

Because of the power of her throw and the height of the arc, when the globule lands, it creates a small crater that sprays earth (EARTH again) into your neighbour's garden.

In this fantasy you imagine that your neighbour is a little (it's a little planet), red-faced (it's a red planet), angry and war-like character clearly carrying a chocolate bar in his hand. Who is this God of War? MARS.

Mars is furious that the earth has gone into his garden and is just about to attack you when, striding on to the scene, comes a giant so large and powerful that he shakes the very foundations (you feel it) of where you are.

See him standing as tall as a giant, and make him as real as you made Venus. He tells Mars to calm down, which Mars immediately does, for this new giant, with a giant cow-lick 'J' on his forehead, is your best friend as well as being the king of the gods – the fifth and largest planet by far: JUPITER.

As you look all the way up to Jupiter's face, way up high, you see the word 'SUN' emblazoned in flashing gold letters across the giant T-shirt on his enormous chest. Each of these gigantic letters stands for the first letter of each of the next three giant planets of the solar system: SATURN, URANUS, NEPTUNE.

Sitting on Jupiter's head, barking his little heart out as he is laughing because he thinks the episode has been so hilarious, is a little (little because this dwarf planet is so small; it is the one that has been downgraded) Walt Disney dog by the name of PLUTO.

Rerun this fantasy in your mind, then see how difficult it is to forget!

In the continuing studies of people's memorisation of the planets, it was found that, before memorising them using the memory principles:

- 800 out of 1000 people didn't really care about the planets and seldom paid attention to information about them.

- 100 out of 1000 felt interested in the planets.

- 100 out of 1000 were actively uninterested and/or disliked the planets.

After memorising the planets using their imagination and the link system, however, virtually every one of the 1000 became actively interested in the planets.

This ongoing study illustrates the very significant fact that if your brain receives data that is rapidly forgotten or it becomes confused, it will reject further data about that subject area. As time goes on, the more information is presented to the brain in the given area, the more it will block that information and the less it will learn, often eventually blocking such information altogether.

If your brain, however, holds information in an organised and memorable matrix, each new bit of information will automatically link to the existing information, naturally building into the patterns of recognition, understanding and memory that we call knowledge.

For example, if you hear that a space probe has been sent to Venus and you do not know where Venus lies within the solar system, the first thing your brain will be confronted with is confusion. You will not know which way the probe has gone from the Earth, whether Venus is hot or cold, what its relationship is to the Sun and why anyone should send a space probe there in the first place. Consequently, you will react by rejecting the information.

If, instead, you know that Venus is the second planet from the Sun and is the one inside Earth's orbit, nearest to Earth, you will know that, as the space probe goes to Venus, it will be going to a planet that is nearer to the Sun and therefore hotter than Earth. Your mind will therefore have a mental image of direction, temperature and nearness to Earth, so will automatically make appropriate associations. At the same time as your mind is doing this, it will also be confirming your knowledge of the other planets. Thus, the more you know, and remember, the more easily and automatically you begin to know more.

Thus, you quickly come to realise that the more structured knowledge you have in your memory, especially if it is in matrix form, the easier it is to remember more. Your memory is so extraordinary that, once given these basic matrices, it will continue to link new information to them without conscious effort on your part.

Conversely, if you do not have basic memory and knowledge structures, the more your mind confronts knowledge, the more it disconnects from it, leaving you with a growing 'memory of all that you have forgotten and not learnt'!

Thus, if you use your memory well, you can look forward to a life of increasing memory skills, expanding knowledge, accelerating ease of learning and, as a consequence of all these, greater mastery of your memory and greater fun.

You have just completed a 'thought experiment' that used techniques identical to those used by the great geniuses throughout history. As soon as you phone or meet a friend or family member, teach them what you have just learnt – it will be an excellent review for you, will 'stamp' the memory more firmly in your brain and give them a useful gift. Encourage them to do the same and, within a few years, you will have initiated that which will enable everybody on Earth to know where Earth is!

Go back now and practise the link system on a couple of lists of your own devising, making sure that you use the memory principles throughout – the more imaginative, absurd and sensual you can be, the better. When you have practised the link system a little, move on to the next chapter.

The number-shape system

In Chapter 4, you learned the link system, applying all the 12 memory techniques with the exception of number and order. We now move on to the first of the peg memory systems.

Peg systems

A 'peg system' is similar to a link system, but differs from it in using a special list of key memory images that never change and to which everything you wish to remember can be linked and associated.

A peg system can be thought of much like a wardrobe containing a certain definite number of hangers on which you hang your clothes. The hangers themselves never change, but the clothes that are hung on them vary infinitely.

How the number-shape system works

In the number-shape system, which is the first of the peg systems covered in this book, the number and shape are the hangers and the things you wish to remember with the system are the clothes to be hung on the hangers. The system is an easy one and uses only the numbers from 1 to 10.

The best system is one you create yourself, rather than one supplied by someone else. that is because minds are infinitely varied, so the associations and images you may have will generally be different from mine and everyone else's. Importantly, the associations and images you generate from your own creative imagination will last far longer and be much more effective for you than any that could be 'implanted'. I shall, however, provide a generic list for the numbers 1 to 10 to get you started, explaining exactly how you can then construct a system yourself. I shall then give examples of how to use it in practice.

In the number-shape system, all you have to do is think of images for each of the numbers from 1 to 10, each image reminding you of the number because both the image and the number have the same shape. For example, the key number-shape memory word that most people use for the number 2 is swan because the number 2 is shaped like a swan and a swan looks like a living, elegant version of the number 2. Another image that 'looks like' the number is an hourglass for the number 8.

The numbers from 1 to 10 are listed below with a suggested image to associate with each number and a blank space for you to pencil in the various words that you think best conjure up the shapes of the numbers. As you select your words, try to make sure that they are exceptionally good visual images, with lots of good colour and basic imagination potential within them. They should be images to which you will be able to link the things you wish to remember with ease and enjoyment, using the SMASHIN' SCOPE of your memory.

In the Number-Shape System, images that 'look like' the number are used as hangers, or hooks, on which to link items you wish to remember. For example, a common Key Image for the number 2 is a swan. 4 is a boat and 8 is an hour glass

Give yourself not more than ten minutes to complete the list from 1 to 10 and, even if you find some numbers difficult, don't worry; just read on:

Number	Generic	Your own words
1	Paintbrush	
2	Swan	
3	Heart	
4	Yacht	
5	Hook	
6	Elephant's trunk	
7	Cliff	
8	Hourglass	
9	Balloon on a stick	
10	Bat and ball	

You can copy the examples shown on page 60. When generating your own number images, try to select the number-shape key memory image for each number that is the best one for you.

When you have done this, use the empty numbered boxes that follow and draw in an appropriate image for each number. (Don't feel inhibited if you consider that you are not good at art; your right brain needs the practice.) Also, the more colours you can use in your images, the better.

Number-shape memory test

When you reach the end of this paragraph, close your eyes and test yourself by mentally running through the numbers from 1 to 10 in order. As you come to each number, mentally link it with the number-shape key image you have selected and drawn.

1	6
2	7
3	8
4	9
5	10

Make sure that you actually see the images on the 'wide plasma screen' of your closed eyelids and/or hear, experience, taste or smell them.

When you have done this exercise once, run through the numbers in reverse order, again linking them with your chosen words and again applying the 12 memory techniques.

Next, pick out numbers randomly and, as quickly as you can, recall your images, making a game to see just how quickly each image comes to mind.

Finally, reverse the whole process by flashing the images on your internal plasma screen, seeing how quickly you can connect the basic numbers to your images. Do this exercise now.

You have already accomplished a memory feat most people would find difficult. You have forged into your memory and creative imagination a system you will be able to use throughout your life – one that combines the qualities of both the left and right hemispheres of your brain.

Using the system is simple and enjoyable and involves the major memory principles of linking/association and imagination. For example, if you have a list of ten items that you wish to remember not simply by linking, as in the previous chapter, but in numerical order, reverse numerical order and random numerical order, the number-shape system makes the whole process easy.

Assume that you wish to remember the following list of items:

1 symphony

2 prayer

3 watermelon

4 volcano

5 motorcycle

6 sunshine

7 apple pie

8 blossoms

9 spaceship

10 field of wheat.

To remember these items in any order, all you have to do is link them with the appropriate number-shape memory image.

Allow yourself no more than three minutes to complete your memorisation of these ten items, using the number-shape system, then write your answers in the table.

Fill in both your number-shape image words *and* the items you were asked to remember for each number. If you feel confident, start now; if not, you may find it helpful to first read the examples given further below.

	Peg word	Item
1		
2		
3		
4		
5		
6		
7		
8		
9		
10		

As a guide for those who might have a little difficulty with this exercise, the following are examples of possible ways in which the ten items to be memorised could be linked to the number-shape key memory images.

1 For *symphony*, you might have imagined a conductor conducting frantically with a gigantic paintbrush, splattering paint over most of the musicians. Alternatively, you might have imagined all the violinists playing their instruments with straws or them all with gigantic penises. Whatever your image, the 12 memory techniques should be applied.

2   *Prayer* is an abstract word. It is often mistakenly assumed that abstract words are hard to memorise. Using proper memory techniques, though, you will find that this is not the case – indeed, you may have already discovered this yourself. All you have to do is to 'image' the abstract in concrete form. You might have to imagine your swan or duck or goose with its wings upheld like hands in prayer or else fill an imaginary church with imaginary swans, geese or ducks, being led in a prayer service by a minister who is also a bird.

3   Easy!

4   You might have imagined your gigantic *volcano* beneath the ocean, seeing it erupting red lava furiously beneath your yacht, the steam and hissing created by the volcano actually heaving your yacht right up from the surface of the water: You might instead, have miniaturised your volcano and placed it on a chair on which you were about to sit (you would certainly feel it if you sat down) or imagined a mountainous table actually blocking the power of the volcano.

5   A giant hook might have come down from the sky and lifted you and your *motorcycle* off the road you were speeding along; or, on your motorcycle, you might have driven, incredibly noisily and disruptively, into a musical instrument shop, knocking over cymbals and drums. Another possibility is to imagine, seated astride the motorcycle, an enormous pregnant woman.

6   Your number-shape key memory image could be pouring out of an elephant's trunk or you might have flung the golf club rhythmically up into the air and it got entangled in a sunbeam that is part of bright *sunshine* so it is being drawn towards the sun. The sunbeam could, instead, be zapping like a laser into a cherry, making it grow gigantic before your very eyes, and you imagine the taste as you bite into it, the juices dribbling down your chin.

7   Your gigantic cliff could actually be made entirely of *apple pie* or your fishing line could catch, instead of a fish, a bedraggled,

soggy apple pie that is, nevertheless, absolutely scrumptious. Another option is that your boomerang could fly off into the distance and, with a thunk, end up in an apple pie as big as a mountain, not returning to you but sending only the delicious aroma of the apple and the pastry.

8   Your snowman could be decorated entirely with exquisite pink *blossoms* or your hourglass could tell the time not by the falling of sand but by the gentle falling of millions of tiny blossoms within the hourglass. Alternatively, your shapely woman could be walking provocatively through endless fields of waist-high fallen blossoms.

9   You could miniaturise your *spaceship* and make it into a balloon and stick. You could also miniaturise it even further and have it as the leading sperm about to fertilise an egg or imagine the spaceship leaving the Earth's atmosphere with a huge flag on its nose.

10 You feel the shock in your bat as it makes contact with the ball, and you see the ball sailing over endless *fields of* rhythmically waving, beautifully golden *wheat.* Another possibility is to imagine Laurel and Hardy playing the ultimate fools and thrashing around, tramping the same endless fields of wheat.

These are, of course, examples and are included to indicate the kind of exaggeration, imagination, sensuality and creative thinking that is necessary to establish the most effective memory pegs.

As with the link system, it is essential that you practise this system on your own. I recommend giving yourself at least one test before you move onto the next chapter.

One of the best ways to do this is to check yourself with members of your family or friends. Ask them to make up a list of any ten items and read the list to you with about a five- to ten-second pause between each item. The instant they have given you the item to be memorised, make the wildest, most colourful and exaggerated associations possible, projecting your images on to your internal screen, and thus consolidating them as you progress. You (and they) will be amazed at the ease with which you can remember the items. It is even more impressive when you are able to repeat them in reverse and random order.

Don't worry about confusing previous lists of items with new ones. As mentioned at the beginning of the chapter, this particular peg system can be compared to hangers – you simply remove one image and replace it with another.

In the next chapter I shall introduce a second system based on the numbers 1 to 10: the number-rhyme system. These two systems can then be combined to enable you to remember 20 items with as much ease as you have just remembered 10.

In subsequent chapters, more sophisticated systems are introduced to allow you to store lists of items stretching into the thousands. Those systems are recommended for long-term memory – the things you wish to retain over a long period of time. The number-shape system you have just learned and the number-rhyme system you are about to learn are recommended for your short-term memory purposes – for those items you wish to remember for only a few hours.

Give yourself about a day or two to become skilled in using the techniques you have learned so far before moving onto the next chapter.

The number-rhyme system

You will find the number-rhyme system especially easy to learn, since it is identical in principle to the number-shape system. Also, like the number-shape system, it can be used for remembering short lists of items that you need to store in your memory for only a brief time.

How the number-rhyme system works

In the number-rhyme system you use the numbers from 1 to 10 again, but, instead of having key memory images of things that resemble the shape of the number, you devise key memory images for words that rhyme with the sounds of the words for the numbers. For example, the key rhyming memory image word that most people use for the number five is 'hive' and the images conjured up for it range from one enormous hive, from which emanates a sky-covering swarm of monster bees, to a microscopic hive, with only one, tiny bee.

As with the link system and the number-shape system, it is essential to apply the 12 memory techniques, making each image as imaginative, colourful and sensual as you possibly can. Below, as before, is a list of the numbers from one to ten, with a blank beside each for you to write in a rhyming image word that you think will produce the best image in your mind for each number. Make sure that the images will be good memory hooks for you. You can also select words from the list of suggestions listed further below.

By now your associative and creative thinking abilities will have improved your mental capacity, so give yourself not ten minutes as before but half that time to fill in your initial key image words below.

Number	Your own words
One	
Two	
Three	
Four	
Five	
Six	
Seven	
Eight	
Nine	
Ten	

As before, I am going to offer a few commonly used image ideas. Consider these and your own key rhyming image words and select for each number, from one to ten, the one you consider to be best for you:

- One: bun, sun, nun, Hun, run, fun
- Two: shoe, pew, loo, crew, gnu, coo, moo
- Three: tree, flea, sea, knee, see, free
- Four: door, moor, boar, paw, pour
- Five: hive, drive, chive, dive, jive
- Six: sticks, bricks, wicks, kicks, licks
- Seven: heaven, Devon, leaven
- Eight: skate, bait, gate, ate, date
- Nine: vine, wine, twine, line, dine, pine
- Ten: hen, pen, den, wren, men, yen.

Having chosen the most appropriate key rhyming image words, draw your images in the spaces provided on page 72, using as much imagination and colour as possible.

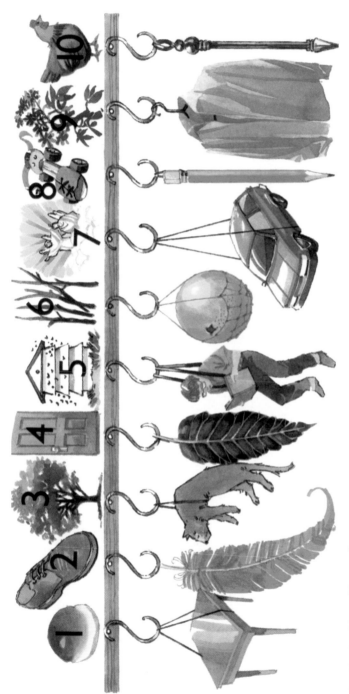

The Number-Rhyme Memory System

1	6
2	7
3	8
4	9
5	10

The Memory Book

Number-rhyme memory test

After you have finished reading this paragraph, test yourself on your chosen key rhyming images. Close your eyes and run through the numbers from one to ten, projecting on to your inner screen a clear and brilliant picture of each key rhyming image you have for each number.

First, run through the list from one to ten in the usual numerical order. Next, run through it in reverse order. Then think of the numbers and images in random order. Finally, pick the images 'out of the air' and connect 'their' numbers to them.

As you do each of these exercises, repeat them, making each repetition faster than the previous one, until you acquire such skill that your mind will instantaneously produce the image as soon as you think of the number.

Spend at least five minutes on this exercise … starting now.

Number-shape and number-rhyme memory test

Now that you have mastered the number-rhyme system, you will see that it can be used in exactly the same way as the number-shape system. Having learned both these systems, you have two separate 1 to 10 (or one to ten) systems, and also the makings of a system that allows you to remember 20 objects in standard, reverse and random sequences. All you have to do is establish one of these two systems as the numbers from 1 to 10, letting the other system represent the numbers from 11 to 20. Decide which system you want to be which and immediately put it to the test!

Give yourself about five minutes to memorise the list below. When your time is up, fill in the answers as explained in the paragraph below the list.

1 Atom

2 Tree

3 Stethoscope

4 Sofa

5 Alley

6 Tile

7 Windscreen

8 Honey

9 Brush

10 Toothpaste

11 Glitter

12 Heater

13 Railway

14 Lighter

15 Wart

16 Star

17 Peace

18 Button

19 Pram

20 Pump

Below are three columns of 20 numbers. The first column follows the standard sequence, the second is in reverse order, the third in random order. Complete each list, filling in next to the number the appropriate item from the list you have just memorized, covering the previous list(s) with your hand or paper as you complete them and start on the next. When you have finished, calculate your score out of a possible 60 points.

1 _____	20 _____	11 _____
2 _____	19 _____	15 _____
3 _____	18 _____	10 _____
4 _____	17 _____	3 _____

5 _____	16 _____	17 _____
6 _____	15 _____	20 _____
7 _____	14 _____	4 _____
8 _____	13 _____	9 _____
9 _____	12 _____	5 _____
10 _____	11 _____	19 _____
11 _____	10 _____	8 _____
12 _____	9 _____	13 _____
13 _____	8 _____	1 _____
14 _____	7 _____	18 _____
15 _____	6 _____	7 _____
16 _____	5 _____	16 _____
17 _____	4 _____	6 _____
18 _____	3 _____	12 _____
19 _____	2 _____	2 _____
20 _____	1 _____	14 _____

Score, out of 60 points:..........

If at first it doesn't work perfectly . . .

You will almost certainly have improved on your performance in the original test, but you might find that you are still having difficulty with certain associations. Check any such 'weak' associations and examine the reasons for any failure. These will usually include:

- they are associations that you don't like;

- the associations are too close or too similar to each other;

- not enough exaggeration and imagination;

- not enough colour;

- not enough movement;

- weak links;

- not enough sensuality;

- not enough humour.

Take courage from the fact that the more you practise, the more such weak links will become a matter of history. Today and tomorrow, test yourself whenever possible. Ask as many of your friends and acquaintances as you can to challenge you on lists that they make up for you to remember.

On the first few attempts, you may make the odd error, even so, you will be performing far beyond the average. Consider any errors and mistakes you make to be good opportunities for examining – and subsequently strengthening – any areas of weakness in your memory systems and the way you apply them. If you persevere, you will soon be able to fire back lists given to you, without any hesitation and without any fear of failure. You will then be able to use the systems confidently – for pleasure, for entertainment, practical purposes, and exercising your general memory 'muscle'.

As you become more skilled, keep a continuing and growing Mind Map of the areas in your life where you apply the systems you are currently learning.

In the next chapter you will learn a basic system used and developed by those masters of mnemonics, the Romans.

The Roman room/memory palace system

The Romans were great inventors and practitioners of mnemonic techniques, one of their most popular being the 'Roman room'. This is basically a variation on the 'method of loci' memory technique, which dates back further, to the Ancient Greeks – 'loci' meaning place.

With little writing material available, it was common for orators and others to memorise their speeches or other items by imagining a journey and then mentally tracing their steps to recall each article. Imagination, association and location were the memory triggers.

Most memory systems hark back to the 'loci' method. It's tried and tested (not least by eight times World Memory Champion Dominic O'Brien).

Imagine this imaginary room

The Romans constructed their memory system easily. They imagined the entrance to their house and their room and then filled the room with as many objects and items of furniture as they chose – each object and piece of furniture serving as a link image, to which they attached the things they wished to remember. The Romans were particularly careful not to make a mental rubbish dump of their rooms; precision and order (attributes of the left side of your brain) are essential to the success of this system.

A Roman might, for example, have constructed his imaginary entrance and room with two gigantic pillars at either side of the front door, a carved lion's head as his doorknob and an exquisite statue on the immediate left as he walked in. Next to the statue might have been a large sofa covered with the fur of one of the animals the Roman had hunted, next to the sofa a flowering plant and, in front of the sofa, a large marble table on which were placed goblets, a wine container, a bowl of fruit and the like.

Let's say that the Roman then wished to remember to:

1 buy a pair of sandals

2 get his sword sharpened

3 buy a new servant

4 tend to his grapevine

5 polish his helmet

6 buy a present for his child.

He would simply imagine (see illustration opposite):

1 the first pillar at the entrance of his imaginary room festooned with thousands of sandals, the leather polished and glistening, and the smell delighting his nostrils

2 sharpening his sword on the right-hand pillar, hearing the scraping as he did so and feeling the blade as it became sharper and sharper

3 his new servant riding a roaring lion

4 his exquisite statue totally entwined with a grapevine on which were luscious grapes that he could see and taste so well in his mind that he would actually salivate;

5 his helmet as a substitute container for his imaginary flowering plant;

6 himself on his sofa, his arm around the child for whom he wishes to buy a gift.

An example of the Roman room system (see text opposite).

The Roman room system is particularly amenable to the application of the strengths of the left and right hemispheres of your brain, and the 12 memory techniques, because it requires very precise structuring and ordering, as well as a lot of imagination and sensuality.

The delight of this system is that the room can be entirely imaginary, so you can have in it every wonderful item that you wish: things that please all your senses, items of furniture and objects of art you have always desired to possess in real life and, similarly, foods and decorations that especially appeal to you. Another major advantage of using this system is that, if you begin to imagine yourself in possession of certain items that exist in your imaginary room, both your memory and creative intelligence will begin to work paraconsciously on ways in which you can actually acquire such objects in real life, increasing the probability that you will eventually do so.

Your Roman room

The Roman room system eliminates all boundaries on your imagination and allows you to remember as many items as you wish. On a piece of paper jot down quickly your first thoughts on the items that you would like to have in your own room, the shape and design of the room. When you have completed this, draw your ideal memory room (on a separate sheet of paper), either as an artist's drawing or architect's plan, drawing and writing in the names of items with which you are going to furnish and decorate it.

First, select ten specific 'loci' or locations for your memory items, building up to 20, 30, 50, adding rooms to your house (or your castle, village, city, country, galaxy or universe!) The 'journey' around your room can be expanded into a journey around your favourite building, holiday spot or where you live.

If you are especially imaginative and combine this with romanticism, you might wish to create a Memory Palace. This is exactly the same as a Roman Room expanded into a Roman Mansion, and has the added advantage of creating in your mind a fantastical and architectural masterpiece of imagination and memory.

Many people, including memory champions, find this is their favourite memory system. The first and eight times World Memory Champion Dominic O'Brien uses Roman rooms, routes and Mind Maps in his memory competitions. They use enormous sheets of paper so that they can include hundreds of items in a gigantic room. If you wish to do this, by all means do so.

When you have completed this task, take a number of 'mental walks' around your room, memorising precisely the order, position and number of items in the room and, similarly, sensing with all your senses the colours, tastes, textures, smells, scents or aromas and sounds within your room, using the whole range of your brain's abilities.

As with the previous memory systems you have learned, practise memorising using the Roman room system both alone and with friends until the system is a firmly established technique. Then, turn to the next chapter to try out the alphabet system – a variation on the techniques you have just learned.

The alphabet
system

The alphabet system is the final peg system described in *The Memory Book* and is similar in construction to the number-shape and number-rhyme systems. The only difference is that, instead of using numbers, it uses the letters of the alphabet.

As with all the other memory systems, the 12 memory techniques are used to enable the alphabet system to work as effectively as it does.

The rules for constructing your alphabet memory system are simple:

● select a key memory image word that starts with the *sound* of each letter

● make sure the word is easy to remember

● make sure the word is easy to imagine

● make sure the word is simple to draw.

If you can think of several possibilities for a letter, use the one that comes first in the dictionary. For example, for the letter '*L*' it would be possible to use '*elastic*', '*elegy*', '*elephant*', '*elbow*', and '*elm*'. If you were looking up those words in the dictionary, the first one you would come to would be elastic, so that would be the word you would select for your alphabet system.

The reason for this rule is that, if you should ever forget your alphabet key image word, you can mentally flick through the letters of the alphabet in order, rapidly arriving at the correct word. In the example given, if you had forgotten your alphabet system image for the letter 'L', you would try 'ela ...' and would then immediately recall your key image word, '*elastic*'.

If the letter itself makes a word when you say it (for example, '*I*' makes the word '*eye*', and '*J*' makes the word *jay*, the bird), then that is the word you should use. In some cases, it is possible to use meaningful initials instead of complete words – for example, '*UN*' for '*U*'.

Opposite is a table listing the letters of the alphabet. Paying close attention to the rules for constructing your alphabet system outlined above, pencil in your own initial alphabet system image words in the spaces provided, after looking at the table with suggested words that follow this table.

When you have completed your initial thoughts, recheck your alphabet image words, making sure that you have started your words with the *sound* of the letter or they are words made by saying the sound of the letter, not simply by the letter itself. For example, 'ant', 'bottle', 'case', 'dog' and 'eddy' would not be correct alphabet system image words because they do not start with the sound of the letter as it is pronounced when you are reciting the alphabet.

Having rechecked your own words, compare them with the suggestions given in the second table, and, when you have done so, select your final list and draw your images for them in the blank squares on pages 87–9.

When you have completed your alphabet image word drawings, review them in exactly the same way as you have the previous memory systems, mentally visualising them in standard order, reverse order and random order. Similarly, make sure you test the system on your own, then with family or friends.

Letter	Your own alphabet image words
A	
B	
C	
D	
E	
F	
G	
H	
I	
J	
K	
L	
M	
N	
O	
P	
Q	
R	
S	
T	
U	
V	
W	
X	
Y	
Z	

Letter	Suggested alphabet image words
A	Ace
B	Bee (sounding the letter itself makes a word – such a word should be used in all cases)
C	Sea (the same rule applies)
D	Deed (legal – the initials DDT may be preferred)
E	Easel
F	Effervescence
G	Jeep or jeans
H	H-bomb
I	Eye
J	Jay (as before, the sound saying the letter makes)
K	Cake
L	Elastic (or 'elbow', if you pronounce 'elastic' with a long 'e')
M	MC (emcee)
N	Enamel (or 'entire', if you pronounce 'enamel' with a long e)
O	Oboe
P	Pea
Q	Queue
R	Arch
S	Eskimo
T	Tea (or perhaps T-square)
U	Yew
V	Vehicle (or the initials VIP)
W	WC
X	X-ray
Y	Wife
Z	Zebra

A

B

C

D

E

F

G

H

I

J

K

L

M

N

O

P

Q

R

S

T

The Memory Book

Double your memory power

You have now learned the five introductory memory systems: link, number-shape, number-rhyme, Roman room and alphabet. Each of the five systems can be used either independently or in conjunction with another system. Furthermore, one or two of the systems of your choice can be set aside, if you wish, as constant memory banks if you have certain lists or orders of items that you will need to be able to recall over a period of a year or more.

Icecubes

Before moving on to the broader systems, I want to introduce you to a simple and intriguing method for instantly doubling the capacity of any of the systems you have learned so far.

When you have reached the end of a system but wish to add further associations, all you have to do is go back to the beginning of your system and imagine your association word exactly as you usually imagine it, but as if it were contained in a huge block of ice. This simple visualisation technique will drastically change the association pictures you have formed and will double the effectiveness of your system by giving you the original list *plus* that list in its new context.

The ice factor in action

If your first key in the number-shape system was paintbrush, you would imagine that same paintbrush either buried in the heart of your giant block of ice or protruding from the corners or sides.

If your first word in the number-rhyme system was '*bun*', then you could imagine a hot bun melting the edges of the ice block in which it was contained.

If your first word in the alphabet system was '*ace*', then you could imagine a giant playing card either frozen in the centre or forming one of the six sides of an ice block.

If, therefore, you were using your 'second' alphabet system (the alphabet in a huge block of ice) and the first item you wanted to remember was '*parrot*', you might imagine your parrot crashing through the centre heart, spade, club or diamond of your card, shattering the ice block, with lots of squawking and cracking going on.

You have now learned the introductory, basic Link and Peg Memory Systems. You now have the ability to remember randomly linked items, two sets of ten items, a large number of ordered items (with your Roman room) and 26 ordered items. You can also instantly double that capacity by using the 'ice cube' method.

From here on you will be learning more advanced, expansive and sophisticated systems that will enable you to remember dates, names and faces, dreams and lists of hundreds even thousands, of items.

In the next section, we explore the 'major system' of memory on which a limitless series of other memory systems can be built and then used to tackle memory blockers such as telephone numbers, anniversary or history dates and vocabulary.

I have **memorised** over 3000 words from Ernest Hemingway's *The Old Man and the Sea* and each word's **numerical position**. If you ask me the 6th word on line 15 on page 8, **I can name it**.

Creighton Carvello, who inspired Dominic O'Brien and the Modern Memory Records Phenomenon

Part 3
The advanced systems

Part 3 explains how to supercharge your memory banks using the 'major system' – a fantastic memory technique that enables you to recall thousands and even tens of thousands of items of data, from numbers on playing cards, to telephone numbers, personal diary dates and historical dates and vocabulary.

The major system

So far you have learned and practised the essential linking and pegging systems to boost your memory and remember lists of objects in the tens and twenties. Now it's time to take on the ultimate basic memory system. It is both flexible and limitless and will enable you to remember numbers and dates, and order and structure memory in hundreds and thousands of detailed ways.

It is called the 'major system' and it was introduced by Stanislaus Mink von Wennsshein. It has been used and continually improved for almost 400 years.

The major system's special code

The basic concept of the system is that it makes use of a different consonant or consonant sound for each number from 0 to 9 using a special code.

Number = associated code
0   = s, z, soft c
1   = d, t, th
2   = N
3   = M
4   = R
5   = L
6   = j, sh, soft ch, dg, soft g
7   = k, hard ch, hard c, hard g, ng, qu

8   = f, v

9   = b, p

The vowels a, e, i, o, u and the letters h, w and y do not have numbers associated with them and are used simply as 'blanks' in the key memory image words you will soon be creating. To save you the trouble of remembering them by rote, here are some simple remembering devices:

0 The letter 's', or 'z', is the first sound of the word 'zero', 'o' is the last letter.

1 The letters 'd' and 't' have one downstroke.

2 The letter 'n' has two downstrokes.

3 The letter 'm' has three downstrokes.

4 The letter 'r' is the last letter in the word 'four'.

5 The letter 'l' can be thought of as either the Roman numeral for '50' or an open hand, the index finger and thumb forming an 'L' shape.

6 The letter 'j' is the mirror image of '6'.

7 The letter 'k', when seen as a capital, contains five number '7's.

8 The letter 'f', when handwritten, has two loops, similar to the number '8'.

9 The letters 'b' and 'p' are the mirror image of '9'.

As with the number-rhyme and number-shape systems, your task is to create a key memory image word that can be immediately and permanently linked with the number it represents. Take, for example, the number 1. You have to think of a memory image word that creates a good visual image and contains only 'd', 't' or 'th' and a vowel sound. Examples include 'day', 'tea', 'toe' and 'the'. When recalling the word chosen for number 1, let's say 'day', you would know that it could represent only the number 1 because the consonant letter in the word represents no other number and vowels count only as blanks in this system.

Try another example: the number 34. In this case, the number 3 is represented by the letter 'm', and 4 is represented by the letter 'r'. Examples of possible words include 'mare', 'more', 'moor' and 'mire'. In selecting the 'best' word for this number, you once again make use of the alphabet order to assist both in choice of word and in recall – in other words, the letters you have to choose are 'm' and 'r' so you simply mentally run through the vowels a, e, i, o, u, using the first vowel that enables you to make an adequate memory word. The case in question is easily solved, since 'a' fits between 'm' and 'r' to direct you towards the word 'mare'.

The advantage of using this alphabet order system is that, should a word in the major system ever be forgotten, it can actually be 'worked out' from the basic information. All you have to do is place the letters of the number in their correct order and then 'slot in', in order, the vowels. As soon as you touch the correct combination, your memory image word will immediately come to mind.

Initial major system exercise

First, letting the letter 'd' represent in each case the '1' of the number, try to complete the words for numbers 10 to 19 in the table below using the alphabet order system for these numbers.

Don't worry if this exercise proves a little difficult – following the table is a complete list of memory image words for the numbers 0 to 100. Don't just accept them, though – check each one carefully, changing any that you find difficult to visualise or for which you have a better substitute.

Use a strong noun or verb as it creates a good memory image on which to hang your information.

Number	Letters	Words
10		
11		
12		
13		
14		
15		
16		
17		
18		
19		

Initial 101 memory image words for the major system

0	Saw	34	Mare	68	Chaff
1	Day	35	Mail	69	Chap
2	Noah	36	Mash	70	Case
3	Ma	37	Mac	71	Cat
4	Ra	38	Mafia	72	Can
5	Law	39	Map	73	Cameo
6	Jaw	40	Race	74	Car
7	Key	41	Rat	75	Call
8	Fee	42	Rain	76	Cage
9	Bay	43	Ram	77	Cake
10	Daze	44	Ra-ra	78	Café
11	Dad	45	Rail	79	Cab
12	Dan	46	Rage	80	Face
13	Dam	47	Rack	81	Fad
14	Dairy	48	Rafia	82	Fan
15	Dale	49	Rap	83	Fame
16	Dash	50	Lace	84	Fair
17	Deck	51	Lad	85	Fall
18	Daffy	52	Lane	86	Fish
19	Dab	53	Lamb	87	Fag
20	NASA	54	Lair	88	Fife
21	Net	55	Lily	89	Fab
22	Nan	56	Lash	90	Base
23	Name	57	Lake	91	Bat
24	Nero	58	Laugh	92	Ban
25	Nail	59	Lab	93	Bam!
26	Niche	60	Chase	94	Bar
27	Nag	61	Chat	95	Ball
28	Navy	62	Chain	96	Bash
29	Nab	63	Chime	97	Back
30	Mace	64	Chair	98	Beef
31	Mat	65	Cello	99	Babe
32	Man	66	Cha-cha	100	Daisies
33	Ma'am	67	Check		

You now possess the code and keys to a peg memory system for the numbers from 0 to 100 – a system that contains the pattern for its own memorisation. As you have seen, this system is limitless. In other words, now that you have letters for the numbers 0 to 9, it should be possible for you to devise key image words for the numbers not only 0 to 100 but also 100 to 1000. This system could, of course, go on forever. For those of you who wish to do this, I have developed a system named SEM[3] (the self-enhancing master memory matrix), which is outlined in detail in Part 4.

Devising your own memory image words for numbers 101 to 1000

An alternative method is to stick with making every number into a letter and making a key memory image word from that combination of letters. In the pages that follow I have devised a list of key image words for the numbers 101 to 1000.

After certain of the more difficult words I have included:

- a suggestion for a way in which an image might be formed from the word

- or a dictionary definition of the word, the definition including words or ideas that should help you form your image

- or 'new' definitions for words that place them in a humorous or unusual but certainly more memorable form

The remaining words are followed by blank spaces. In the spaces provided you should write in your own key words for, or ideas about, the images you will be using.

In some cases, where the combination of letters makes the use of single words difficult, double words have been used, such as 'no cash' for the number 276 ('n', hard 'c', 'sh'): in other cases it is necessary to include vowels (which have no numerical meaning) at the beginning of the word – while for example, the number 394 ('m', 'p', 'r') is represented by the word 'empire' – in still other cases, words have been used of which only the first three letters pertain to the number.

Managing the major system when using this method

When expanding your major system beyond 100 in this way, your next task is to check the major system list below carefully. It would obviously be too much to ask you to do this at one sitting, so I suggest the more modest goal of checking, making images for and remembering ten items each day.

As you go through the list, attempt to make your images of the words as solid as you can. Remember that, as you memorise this entire list, you should try to use both sides of your brain, making sure that you are reviewing and consolidating the order, while at the same time increasing and expanding your imagination, creativity and awareness of your senses.

Even when words refer to ideas or concepts, take them to a more concrete level. For example, the number 368, represented by the memory words 'much force', should not be pictured as some vague power or energy in space, it should be an image in which much force is used to accomplish or achieve – for example, a weightlifter at the Olympics. In other words, in each case you will be attempting to make the memory word as pictorial and memorable as possible. Remember the rules in Chapter 3: use your whole SMASHIN' SCOPE.

In cases where words are similar in concept to previous words, it is most important to make your images for them as different as possible. The same caution applies to words that are pluralised because of the addition of 's'. In these cases, imagine a great number of items as opposed to one enormous item. You will find your consolidation of the words in the major system useful because it will enable you to remember the astounding number of 1000 items (in order or randomly) and because it will exercise your creative linking ability, which is so necessary for remembering anything.

A number of the words used as mnemonics in this major system are interesting in their own right. As you check through and memorise each list of 100, have a dictionary by your side to help you if you run into difficulty selecting your key words. In these instances, it will:

- serve as a means of solidifying the images for you

- enable you to select the best possible images or words

- be of value in the improvement of your general vocabulary

- be of value in the improvement of your creativity.

If you have read my book *The Speed Reading Book*, combine, where feasible, the vocabulary exercise included in it with your major system exercise.

Memory image words for numbers 101 to 1000

101	Dust	115	Detail
102	Design	116	Detach
103	Dismay	117	Toothache
104	Desire	118	Dative – a noun case that expresses giving
105	Dazzle		
106	Discharge		
107	Disc		
108	Deceive	119	Deathbed
109	Despair	120	Tennis
110	Dates – the succulent sticky fruit	121	Dent
		122	Denun – to take a nun or nuns away from a place or situation
111	Deadwood – decayed, often twisted, remains of trees		
		123	Denim
		124	Dinner
112	Deaden	125	Downhill
113	Diadem – a crown; a wreath of leaves or flowers worn around the head	126	Danish – native of Denmark
		127	Dank – unpleasantly soaked or damp; marshy or swampy
114	Daughter		

128 Downfall

129 Danube – the river (or picture waltzing to the *Blue Danube*)

130 Demise

131 Domed – having a large, rounded summit, as a head or a church

132 Demon

133 Demimonde – the fringe of society

134 Demure

135 Dimly

136 Damage

137 Democracy

138 Dam full

139 Damp

140 Dress

141 Dart

142 Drain

143 Dram
144 Drawer
145 Drill
146 Dredge – apparatus for bringing up mud (or oysters) from the sea or river bottom
147 Drag
148 Drive
149 Drip
150 De luxe
151 Daylight
152 Delinquent
153 Dilemma – a position in which the choice is usually between two evils
154 Dealer
155 Delilah – temptress of Samson; false and wily woman
156 Deluge – a great flood; Noah's flood
157 Delicacy
158 Delphi – the ancient Greek town where the sanctuary of the oracle was located
159 Tulip

160 Duchess
161 Dashed
162 Dudgeon – state of strong anger, resentment or feeling of offence
163 Dutchman
164 Dodger – a wily, tricky, elusive person
165 Dash light – imagine the dash light in your car
166 Dishwasher
167 Dechoke – reverse the image of choke, either in relation to a car or to strangling someone
168 Dishevel – to make the hair or clothes loose, disordered, 'flung about'
169 Dish up – to serve food
170 Decks
171 Decade
172 Token
173 Decamp – imagine confusion in the dismantling of tents and so on

174 Decree – an order made by an authority demanding some kind of action
175 Ducal – imagine anything similar to or looking like a duke
176 Duckish
177 Decaying
178 Take-off
179 Decapitate
180 Defact
181 Defeat
182 Divan
183 Defame
184 Diver
185 Defile
186 Devotion
187 Edifying
188 Two frisky fillies – imagine them in a field or memorable enclosure
189 Two frightened boys – perhaps being chased by 188!
190 Debase – to lower in character, quality or value
191 Debate
192 Debone – to pick the bones

out of, usually from fish

193 Whitebeam – a tree with long, silvery underleaves

194 Dipper – imagine a big dipper at a fairground

195 Dabble

196 Debauch

197 Dipping – imagine someone being dipped forcibly into water, as in the medieval torture technique

198 Dab off – imagine a stain or blood being dabbed off with cotton wool

199 Depip – to take the pips out of (imagine a pomegranate)

200 Nieces

201 Nasty

202 Insane

203 Noisome – harmful, noxious, smelling awful

204 No sir!

205 Nestle

206 Incision – a clean cutting of something, as with a doctor's scalpel

207 Nosegay – a small bunch of sweetly scented flowers

208 Unsafe

209 Newsboy

210 Notice

211 Needed

212 Indian

213 Anatomy

214 Nadir – the lowest point; place or time of great depression

215 Needle

216 Night watch

217 Antique

218 Native

219 Antibes – a port and resort in south-east France, on the Mediterranean

220 Ninnies – group of people with weak minds, simpletons

221 Ninth – imagine the ninth hole of a golf course

222 Ninon – a lightweight dress fabric

made of silk

223 No name – imagine a person who has forgotten his name

224 Nunnery

225 Union hall

226 Nunnish – pertaining to or like a nun

227 Non-aqua – having nothing at all to do with water

228 Nineveh

229 Ninepin – one of nine upright pieces of wood to be knocked down in the game of ninepins

230 Names

231 Nomad

232 Nominee – a person nominated for a position or office

233 No ma'am

234 Enamour – to charm, to animate with love

235 Animal

236 No mash – imagine a saucepan that

has just been emptied of mashed potatoes

237 Unmake
238 Nymph – a beautiful mythological maiden, always young
239 Numb
240 Nurse
241 Narrate
242 No run
243 Norm – a standard; a set pattern to be maintained
244 Narrower
245 Nearly
246 Nourish
247 New York
248 Nerve
249 Nearby
250 Nails
251 Nailed
252 Nylon
253 New loam – freshly turned rich and fertile soil
254 Kneeler
255 Nail hole
256 Knowledge
257 Nailing
258 Nullify
259 Nailbrush
260 Niches – vertical

recesses in a wall to contain a statue

261 Unshod
262 Nation
263 Unjam
264 Injure
265 Unshell – to extract a living organism from its shell
266 Nosh shop – imagine a corner snackbar or something similar
267 No joke – a joke that falls flat
268 Unshaved
269 Unship – imagine a great crowd of people being ordered off a ship
270 Necks
271 Naked
272 Noggin – a person's head or a small cup or mug
273 Income
274 Anchor
275 Nickel – a grey metal related to cobalt
276 No cash – imagine some-

one fumbling in his pockets in order to pay a restaurant bill

277 Knocking
278 Encave – to confine to a dark place; to keep in a cave
279 Uncap – imagine schoolboys stealing one another's caps
280 Nephews
281 Nevada
282 Uneven
283 Infamy
284 Never
285 Navel
286 Knavish – having the characteristics of a roguish trickster
287 Invoke – to address in prayer; to implore assistance or protection
288 Unfavourable
289 Enfeeble – to make extremely weak and unable to function
290 Nibs

291 Unpod – to take from the pod, as peas

292 New pan – imagine a brilliantly shiny frying pan

293 New beam – imagine the first beam ever from the sun

294 Neighbour

295 Nibble

296 Nippish

297 Unpack

298 Unpaved

299 Nabob – a wealthy person, especially one returned from India with a fortune

300 Moses

301 Mast

302 Mason

303 Museum

304 Miser

305 Missile

306 Massage

307 Mask

308 Massive

309 Mishap

310 Midas – the king who turned everything he touched to gold

311 Midday

312 Maiden

313 Madam

314 Motor

315 Medal

316 Modish – in the current style or fashion

317 Medic

318 Midwife

319 Mudpie

320 Manse – the home of a Presbyterian minister

321 Mend

322 Minion – favourite child, servant or animal; slave

323 Minim – a creature of the smallest size or importance; a musical note

324 Manner

325 Manila

326 Manage

327 Maniac

328 Manful – brave, resolute, bold

329 Monopoly – a popular board game

330 Maims

331 Mammoth

332 Mammon – the Syrian god of riches; worldly wealth

333 My mum

334 Memory

335 Mammal

336 My match

337 Mimic

338 Mummify – to preserve a body by embalming

339 Mump

340 Mars

341 Maraud – to make a plunderous raid; to go about pilfering

342 Marine

343 Miriam

344 Mirror

345 Moral

346 March

347 Mark

348 Morphia – the principal narcotic of opium

349 Marble

350 Males

351 Malt

352 Melon

353 Mile man – a man who runs a mile

354 Miller

355 Molehill

356 Mulish – imagine anything that is characteristic of a mule

357 Milk

358 Mollify – to soften, assuage, appease

359 Mailbag

360 Matches

361 Mashed

362 Machine

363 Mishmash – a jumble, hotch-potch, medley

364 Major

365 Mesh lock – imagine something like a gear cog meshing and locking or a lock that operates by an intricate mesh

366 Magician

367 Magic

368 Much force

369 Much bent

370 Mikes

371 Mocked

372 Mohican

373 Make muck

374 Maker

375 Meekly

376 My cash

377 Making

378 Make off – to hurry away, as a thief from the scene of a crime

379 Magpie

380 Mauve skirt

381 Mufti – an expounder of Mohammedan law; civilian dress as opposed to uniform

382 Muffin

383 Movement

384 Mayfair

385 Muffle

386 My fish

387 Mafeking – a town in South Africa, well known for relief of siege there in 1900

388 Mauve feet

389 Movable

390 Mopes – sulks; being dull or out of spirits

391 Moped

392 Embank – to confine or protect (river, road and so on) by a bank

393 Wampum – name for money beads and shells used by Native American Indians

394 Empire

395 Maple

396 Ambush

397 Impact

398 Mob violence

399 Imbibe – to drink; absorb (often used of liquor)

400 Recess

401 Recite

402 Raisin

403 Résumé – a summing up; a condensed statement; a summary

404 Racer

405 Wrestle

406 Rose show

407 Risk

408 Receive

409 Rasp – to rub with a coarse file; to utter in a grating way

410 Raids

411 Radiate

412 Rattan – Indian climbing palm with a long, thin, pliable stem

413 Redeem

414 Radar – imagine 'beaming in' on some object in the sky

415 Rattle

416 Radish

417 Reading
418 Ratify – to settle, confirm, approve, establish
419 Rat bait
420 Reigns
421 Rained
422 Reunion
423 Uranium – a radioactive white metallic element
424 Runner
425 Runnel – a rivulet or gutter
426 Ranch
427 Rank
428 Run-off – a decisive final contest; a gutter or spillway
429 Rainbow
430 Remus – one of two brothers suckled by a wolf in infancy; he became one of the mythological founders of Rome
431 Rammed
432 Roman
433 Remember
434 Ramrod
435 Rommel – notorious German war leader
436 Rummage
437 Remake
438 Ramify – to form branches, subdivisions or offshoots
439 Ramp
440 Roars
441 Reared
442 Rareness
443 Rear man – the last man in a column or file
444 Rarer
445 Rarely
446 Raree show – a peepshow
447 Rearing
448 Rarefy – to lessen the density or solidity of, especially air
449 Rarebit – a dainty morsel; often applied to Welsh rarebit
450 Release
451 Railed
452 Reloan
453 Realm
454 Roller
455 Reel line – imagine a fishing line tangled on its reel
456 Relish
457 Relic
458 Relief
459 Relapse
460 Riches
461 Reached
462 Region
463 Regime – mode, style, diet; form of government
464 Rasher
465 Rachel
466 Rejudge
467 Raging
468 Arch foe – imagine yourself as a knight with one giant foe among a number of others
469 Reach up
470 Racks
471 Racket
472 Reckon
473 Requiem – a service spoken or sung for the peace of the soul of a dead person
474 Raker – imagine a man who does nothing but rake gardens
475 Recall
476 Roguish

477 Rococo – a highly ornamental, florid style in design
478 Recover
479 Rack up – colloquialism meaning to score points in sport
480 Refuse
481 Raft
482 Raven
483 Revamp – to renovate, revise or improve
484 Reefer – a marijuana cigarette
485 Raffle
486 Ravage
487 Revoke – a card player's failure to follow suit, though he could
488 Revive
489 Rough passage – a crossing over rough sea; a difficult or testing time
490 Rabies
491 Rabid – furious, violent, unreasoning, mad
492 Ribbon

493 Ripe melon
494 Rapier
495 Rabble
496 Rubbish
497 Rebuke
498 Rebuff
499 Republic – a society with equality among members
500 Lasses
501 Last
502 Lesson
503 Lyceum – a place in Athens where Aristotle taught
504 Laser – a super-concentrated beam of light coming from a vibrating substance
505 Lazily
506 Alsatian
507 Lacing
508 Lucifer
509 Lisp
510 Ladies
511 Lighted
512 Latin
513 Late meal
514 Ladder
515 Ladle
516 Old age
517 Leading
518 Old foe

519 Lead pipe
520 Lance
521 Land
522 Linen
523 Liniment
524 Linear
525 Lineal
526 Launch
527 Lank
528 Lunar flight
529 Line-up
530 Looms
531 Limit
532 Layman
533 Lame mare
534 Lamarck – famous French zoologist and botanist
535 Lamella – a thin plate, especially of tissue or bone
536 Lime juice
537 Looming
538 Lymph – a bodily fluid resembling plasma
539 Lamp
540 Layers
541 Lard
542 Learn
543 Alarm
544 Leerer
545 Laurel
546 Large
547 Lark
548 Larva

549 Larrup –
     colloquial for
     'to thrash'
550 Lilies
551 Lilt
552 Lowland
553 Lilo mattress – a
     camping
     mattress that
     serves as a bed
554 Lowlier
555 Lily-livered
556 Low ledge
557 Lilac
558 Low life
559 Lullaby
560 Lashes
561 Legit –
     colloquial for
     that which is
     honest
562 Legion
563 Lush meadow
564 Lecher
565 Lushly
566 All-Jewish
567 Logic
568 Low shove
569 Lush pea
570 Lakes
571 Licked
572 Lagoon
573 Locum –
     colloquial for a
     deputy in any
     office, but
     especially a
     doctor

574 Lacquer
575 Local
576 Luggage
577 Licking
578 Liquefy – to
     bring a solid or
     a gas to a liquid
     condition
579 Lock-up
580 Leaves
581 Livid
582 Elfin – like, or
     relating to, a
     fairy or an elf
583 Alluvium – soil
     deposited or
     washed down
     by the action
     of water
584 Lever
585 Level
586 Lavish
587 Leaving
588 Leave off
589 Lifeboat
590 Lips
591 Leaped
592 Lib now –
     imagine this
     phrase as a
     women's
     liberation
     placard
593 Low bum
594 Labour
595 Label
596 Lip chap – a
     cold sore on
     the lip

597 Lawbook
598 Leapfrog
599 Lap up
600 Chases
601 Chaste
602 Jason – and the
     Golden Fleece
603 Chessman
604 Chaser
605 Chisel
606 Cheese show
607 Chasing
608 Joseph
609 Cheese pie
610 Shades
611 Shaded
612 Showdown
613 Chatham –
     naval dockyard
     town on the
     River Medway,
     Kent
614 Chatter
615 Chattel
616 Chitchat
617 Cheating
618 Shadoof – a
     mechanism for
     raising water,
     consisting of a
     long pole hung
     from a post and
     a bucket, used
     in Egypt
619 Chat up – to talk
     to a person with
     further contact
     in mind

620 Chains
621 Chant
622 Genuine
623 Chinaman
624 Joiner
625 Channel
626 Change
627 Chink – in the armour
628 Geneva – headquarters for certain United Nations organisations; major city in Switzerland
629 Shinbone
630 Chums
631 Ashamed
632 Showman
633 Jemima – boot with elastic sides, having no laces or clasps to fasten
634 Chimera – a fire-breathing monster with a lion's head, a goat's body and a dragon's tail; a fanciful product of the imagination
635 Shameless
636 Jimjams – pyjamas
637 Jamaica

638 Shameful
639 Champ
640 Cheers
641 Chart
642 Shrine
643 Chairman
644 Juror
645 Churl – a surly, ill-bred person
646 Charge
647 Cherokee – Native American Indian
648 Giraffe
649 Chirp
650 Jealous
651 Child
652 Chilean
653 Shalom – salutation at meeting or parting used by Jews
654 Jailer
655 Shallowly – unintellectual, lacking in depth
656 Geology
657 Gelignite
658 Shelf
659 Julep – with mint
660 Judges
661 Judged
662 Jejune – bare, meagre, empty; void of interest
663 Judgement

664 Judger
665 Jewishly
666 Choo-choo-choo – an especially puffy steam engine
667 Joshing – good-natured leg pulling or joking
668 Jehoshaphat – a king of Judah
669 Shoe shop
670 Checks
671 Checked
672 Chicken
673 Checkmate – a position in chess where the opponent's king is trapped; the end of the game
674 Checker
675 Chuckle
676 Check shirt
677 Checking
678 Chekhov – famous Russian author of plays and short stories
679 Jacob
680 Chafes – makes sore or worn by rubbing; irritates
681 Shaft
682 Shaven
683 Chief Mohawk
684 Shaver

685 Joyful

686 Chiffchaff – small European warbler with yellowish-brown plumage

687 Chafing

688 Shove off

689 Shavable

690 Chaps

691 Chapter

692 Japan

693 Jobman

694 Chopper

695 Chapel

696 Sheepish

697 Chipping

698 Sheepfold

699 Shopboy

700 Kisses

701 Cast

702 Casino

703 Chasm

704 Kisser

705 Gazelle

706 Kiss-shy – reluctant to kiss

707 Cask

708 Cohesive – with the quality of sticking together

709 Cusp – the point at which two branches of a curve meet and stop; a pointed end, especially of a crescent moon

710 Cats

711 Cadet

712 Cotton

713 Gotham – a proverbially foolish town

714 Guitar

715 Cattle

716 Cottage

717 Coating

718 Cadaver – a corpse

719 Cut up

720 Cans

721 Canada

722 Cannon

723 Economy

724 Coiner

725 Kennel

726 Conjurer

727 Conk – colloquial for nose or, of a machine, break down

728 Convey

729 Canopy – a covering over a bed or a throne

730 Cameos – pieces of relief carving in stone, agate and so on with layers of colour utilised to give background; small defining role for actor

731 Comet

732 Common

733 Commemorate

734 Camera

735 Camel

736 Game show – as seen on television

737 Comic

738 Comfy

739 Camp

740 Caress

741 Card

742 Corn

743 Cram

744 Career

745 Carol

746 Crash

747 Crack

748 Carafe – a glass water or wine bottle for the dinner table

749 Carp – to find fault; a freshwater fish

750 Class

751 Clod

752 Clan

753 Clam

754 Clear

755 Galileo – Italian astronomer, mathematician and physicist

756 Clash
757 Clack
758 Cliff
759 Clap
760 Cages
761 Caged
762 Cushion
763 Cashmere – expensive and very soft type of yarn, knitted or woven, originally made in Kashmir, India
764 Cashier
765 Cajole – to persuade or soothe by flattery, deceit
766 Quiche shop
767 Catching
768 Cageful
769 Ketchup – tomato sauce
770 Cakes
771 Cooked
772 Cocoon
773 Cucumber
774 Cooker
775 Cackle
776 Quick change – rapid change of costume by an actor and so on to play another part
777 Cooking

778 Quickfire
779 Cock-up – colloquial for messing things up
780 Cafés
781 Cave-dweller
782 Coffin
783 Caveman
784 Caviar
785 Cavil – to raise needless objection
786 Coffee shop
787 Caving
788 Cavafy – poet of Alexandria
789 Coffee-bean
790 Cabs
791 Cupid
792 Cabin
793 Cabman
794 Caper – to frolic, skip or leap lightly, as a lamb; a small berry used for making pickles and condiments
795 Cable
796 Cabbage
797 Coping
798 Keep off
799 Cobweb
800 Faces
801 Fast
802 Pheasant
803 Face mole

804 Visor
805 Facile
806 Visage
807 Facing
808 Face value
809 Face up – colloquial for 'meet the brunt'; accept the challenge or consequences
810 Fates – the three Greek goddesses of destiny
811 Faded
812 Fatten
813 Fathom
814 Fetter
815 Fatal
816 Fattish
817 Fading
818 Fateful
819 Football
820 Fans
821 Faint
822 Finance
823 Venom
824 Fawner – an obsequious or sycophantic person; one who insincerely praises for reward
825 Final
826 Finish

827 Fawning – courting favour by cringing

828 Fanfare

829 Vain boy

830 Famous

831 Vomit

832 Famine

833 Fame-mad

834 Femur – the thigh-bone

835 Female

836 Famish

837 Foaming

838 Fumeful

839 Vamp – adventuress; woman who exploits men; unscrupulous flirt

840 Farce

841 Fort

842 Fern

843 Farm

844 Farrier – a man who shoes horses or treats them for disease

845 Frail

846 Fresh

847 Frock

848 Verify – establish the truth of

849 Verb

850 False

851 Fault

852 Flan

853 Flame

854 Flare

855 Flail – wooden staff at the end of which a short heavy stick hangs, swinging; used for threshing

856 Flash

857 Flake

858 Fluff

859 Flab

860 Fishes

861 Fished

862 Fashion

863 Fishmonger

864 Fisher

865 Facial

866 Fish shop

867 Fishing

868 Fish food

869 Fish bait

870 Focus

871 Faked

872 Fecund – fertile

873 Vacuum

874 Fakir – a Mohammedan or Hindu religious devotee

875 Fickle

876 Fake china

877 Faking

878 Havocful – 'filled' with devastation and destruction

879 Vagabond

880 Fifes

881 Vivid

882 Vivien – Leigh

883 Five a.m.

884 Fever

885 Favillous – consisting of, or pertaining to, ashes

886 Fifish – resembling or having the characteristics of a fife

887 Fifing

888 Vivify – give life to; enliven; animate

889 Viviparous – bringing forth live young rather than eggs

890 Fibs

891 Fibbed

892 Fabian – employing cautious strategy to wear out an enemy

893 Fob-maker

894 Fibre

895 Fable

896 Foppish

897 Fee back – imagine yourself receiving money you had paid for a product that was unsatisfactory

898 Few puffs – imagine someone trying to give up smoking

899 Fab boy – colloquialism for a young boy considered very attractive by girls

900 Basis

901 Pasta

902 Basin

903 Bosom

904 Bazaar

905 Puzzle

906 Beseech – to ask for earnestly; to entreat, supplicate or implore

907 Basic

908 Passive

909 Baseball

910 Beads

911 Bedded

912 Button

913 Bottom

914 Batter

915 Battle

916 Badge

917 Bedding

918 Beautify

919 Bad boy

920 Bans – curses, interdicts, prohibitions, outlawry

921 Band

922 Banana

923 Benumb – to make numb or torpid, insensible or powerless

924 Banner

925 Banal – trivial, trite, stale, commonplace

926 Banish

927 Bank

928 Banff – a holiday resort in north-east Scotland, the Grampians

929 Pin-up

930 Beams

931 Pomade – a scented ointment, originating from apples, to smooth the hair

932 Bemoan – weep or express sorrow for or over; to lament or bewail

933 Beam-maker

934 Be merry

935 Pommel – a rounded knob, especially at the end of a sword-hilt or on a saddle

936 Bombshell

937 Beaming

938 Bumph – derogatory term for direct mail and so on

939 Bump

940 Brass

941 Bread

942 Barn

943 Brim

944 Barrier

945 Barrel

946 Barge

947 Bark

948 Brief

949 Bribe

950 Blaze

951 Bald

952 Balloon

953 Blame

954 Boiler

955 Balliol – one of Oxford University's colleges

956 Blush

957 Black

958 Bailiff – a king's representative in a district; agent of a land-lord; officer under a sheriff

959 Bulb

960 Beaches

961 Budget

962 Passion

963 Pyjamas

964 Poacher – one who trespasses to steal game or fish; a vessel for poaching eggs

965 Bushel – an 8-gallon measure for grain and fruit

966 Pushchair

967 Bushwhacker – backwoods man; guerrilla fighter in the American Civil War

968 Bashful

969 Bishop

970 Bacchus – the Greek god of wine

971 Bucket

972 Bacon

973 Becalm – to still; to make quiet; unable to sail due to lack of wind

974 Baker

975 Buckle

976 Baggage

977 Backing – support, moral or physical; a web of strong material at the back of some woven fabric

978 Back off

979 Back up

980 Beehives

981 Buffet

982 Buffoon – a ludicrous figure; a droll clown

983 Pavement

984 Beaver

985 Baffle

986 Peevish – fretful or irritable

987 Bivouac – a temporary encampment without tents

988 Puffy face

989 Puff up

990 Babies

991 Puppet

992 Baboon

993 Pipe major

994 Paper

995 Babble

996 Baby show

997 Popgun

998 Pipeful

999 Pop-up – an automatic toaster; book with pages parts of which rise when opened to give a three-dimensional effect

1000 These zoos

How to increase everything you have learned so far by 1000 per cent

It is possible, with 10 quick leaps of your imagination, to create a memory system of 1000 from the basic 100 and a memory system of 10,000 from the basic 1000 you have been absorbing above!

To achieve this, use the ice cube method explained near the end of Chapter 8. You simply coat, encase or colour sections of your major system with ice. For each successive 100 you use a different 'substance'. For example, to expand the basic 100 words to 1000 using this new multiplier method, you would adjust the sections of your major system as follows:

100–199   in a block of ice
200–299   covered in thick oil
300–399   in flames
400–499   coloured a brilliant and pulsating purple
500–599   made of beautiful velvet
600–699   completely transparent
700–799   smelling of your favourite fragrance
800–899   placed in the middle of a motorway
900–1000   floating on a single cloud in a beautiful, sunny, clear
           blue sky

To multiply each of these ten 100s by 1000 – thus giving you a total of 10,000 – use the same technique again. For example, by using the colours of the rainbow, you can bathe each of your 1000s in a different colour. Similarly, you could give each 1000 a different look, or a different sound, a different smell, a different taste, a different touch, or a different sensation.

What you choose is up to you, but should be based on whatever gives you the strongest memory impressions.

As with all previous systems, practise the major system privately and with friends. You can probably already begin to sense that the memorisation of books, preparation for examinations and the like will become increasingly easy tasks for you.

If you are interested in pursuing further such super-memory systems, see Part 4 for a detailed introduction to my self-enhancing master memory matrix, or SEM^3 for short.

The applications of the major system are almost as limitless as the system itself and the next chapters of the book will show you how to apply it to the memorisation of cards, long numbers, telephone numbers, dates in history, birthdays and anniversaries and information for examinations.

The card memory system

Now you are ready to use the memory processes you have learned so far to memorise a complete pack of cards. It may take you a few goes but consider the following story.

In 1991, at the time of the first World Memory Championship (WMC) which I founded with Raymond Keene, a shuffled pack of cards could be memorised and recalled accurately by a good contender after around five minutes' cogitation. The original 'memory man', Creighton Carvello, broke the three-minute barrier with a time of 2 minutes 59 seconds in 1987. This inspired Dominic O'Brien to become a master memoriser and eventually world champion.

The task contestants have to master is to memorise, in order, a randomly shuffled pack of cards and, having done so, immediately hand the cards to the adjudicator, raising a hand. So, a competitor has to memorise the entire pack perfectly (in the competition no errors are allowed) and then their hand. In the first WMC after 2 minutes and 29 seconds, Dominic O'Brien's hand shot up as he handed his pack to the adjudicator. After an agonising wait Dominic's adjudicator confirmed he had memorised the entire deck perfectly. Experts promptly pronounced this to be near the limit of human capacity.

Fast forward a decade and a half later, however, and the recall of a complete shuffled pack is down to around 30 seconds. The 30-second barrier in 'speed cards' had been the Holy Grail for any memory athlete for the entire duration of the history of the Mind Sport of Memory.

In 2008, Ben Pridmore smashed even that seemingly unassailable record by 3.72 seconds. It was an unprecedented demolition of what seemed to be the ultimate barrier. It pushed back, to a gigantic degree, the boundaries of human mental capacity. It was the equivalent of Roger Bannister breaking the 'four-minute mile' by 29.76 seconds!

These phenomenal feats increasingly demonstrate that the power of your memory is beyond what the psychologists of memory had predicted would be the limits of human memory and recall.

What is the secret?

The secret to remembering a complete pack of cards is to attach your key memory image for each card to the major system you have learned. All that is necessary to create a key memory image word for each card is to know the first letter of the word for the suit as well as the number of the card in that suit. For example, all words for the club cards will begin with 'c', all words for the hearts with 'h', all words for the spades with 's' and all words for the diamonds with 'd'. The second consonant for the card word will be the consonant represented by the letter from the major system.

Taking as an example the five of spades, you know that it must begin with 's' because it is a spade card and that its last consonant must be 'l' because it is the five, and five in the major system is represented by 'l'. Without much difficulty you arrive at the word 'sale' to represent the five of spades.

Similarly, if you wish to devise a word for the three of diamonds, it must begin with 'd' because it is the diamond suit and its final consonant must be 'm' because the number three is represented by 'm' in the major system. Filling in with the first vowel, you arrive at the word 'dam' as your image word for the three of diamonds.

Memory image words for a standard pack of cards

Following are lists of the cards and their memory image words. A few of the variations will be explained after you have had a chance to familiarise yourself with the list.

Clubs

CA – Cat
C2 – Can
C3 – Cameo
C4 – Car
C5 – Call
C6 – Cash
C7 – Cake
C8 – Café
C9 – Cab
C10 – Case
CJ – Cadet
CQ – Cotton
CK – Club

Diamonds

DA – Day
D2 – Dan
D3 – Dam
D4 – Dare
D5 – Dale
D6 – Dash
D7 – Deck
D8 – Daffy
D9 – Dab
D10 – Daze
DJ – Deadwood
DQ – Deaden
DK – Diamond

Hearts

HA – Hat
H2 – Hen
H3 – Ham
H4 – Hair
H5 – Hail
H6 – Hash
H7 – Hag
H8 – Hoof
H9 – Hub
H10 – Haze
HJ – Headed
HQ – Heathen
HK – Heart

Spades

SA – Sat
S2 – Sin
S3 – Sum
S4 – Sear
S5 – Sale
S6 – Sash
S7 – Sack
S8 – Safe
S9 – Sap
S10 – Seas
SJ – Sated
SQ – Satan
SK – Spade

In this system, aces count as 1, the jacks and queens as 11 and 12, 10 counts as 0, and the king simply as the name of the suit in which he resides. The memory words for the clubs and diamonds are, in many cases, the same as those for the major system words for the seventies and teens, but this need not concern you, as the two lists will never come into conflict.

How does it work?

How do the memory experts dazzle the audience? The answer is quite simple: whenever a card is called out, they associate that card with the appropriate number of the major system.

If, for example, the first card called out is the seven of diamonds they would associate the word 'deck' with the first word of the major system, which is 'day'. They might imagine the entire deck of a boat being bathed in sunlight, making sure that the association is smelled, seen, heard, tasted and touched as much as possible.

If the next card called is the ace of hearts, they would associate the word for that card – 'hat' – with the second word of the major system – 'Noah'. Noah could be imagined standing on the ark, wearing a gigantic rain hat and heavy rain is pouring and splashing down onto it in the most tremendous volume. They could actually imagine that they were Noah, feeling the chill of the water, hearing the splashing and so on.

If the next card called is the queen of spades, they could associate the word for that card – 'Satan' – with the third major system word – 'Ma'. They might imagine their mother in a titanic struggle with Satan in the burning fires of hell, using as much motion, rhythm, colour and sensuality as possible.

Throughout the memorisation of a pack of cards using the major system as the pegs on which to hang the 52 items, you can clearly see that both the logical, analytical, sequential and numerical left side of your brain, and the imaginative, colourful, and rhythmical right side of your brain are being fully utilised. From these few examples, I hope you can see how easy it can be to memorise an entire pack of cards in whatever order they happen to be presented to you. It is a most impressive feat to be able to perform in front of your friends and a cornerstone of the World Memory Championships should you feel bold enough to enter (see Appendix 1).

How to increase your memory further still

Your facility for remembering cards can be taken a step further. It is possible to have someone randomly read you the names of all the cards in the pack, leaving out any six or seven. Without much hesitation, you can name those cards.

There are two ways to do this.

1 The first is to use a technique similar to the link system explained in Chapter 4. Whenever a card is called out, you associate the image word for that card within a larger concept, such as the ice cube previously mentioned. When all the cards have been presented, you simply run down the list of card memory words, noting those words that are not connected with the larger memory concept. For example, if the four of clubs has been called, you might have pictured a car sliding across the huge cube of ice or being trapped within it. You could hardly forget that image. If the four of clubs had *not* been called, however, you would immediately remember that you had nothing to remember for it.

2 The other system for this kind of feat is to mutate, or change, in some way the card memory image word if that card is called. For example, if the king of clubs is called and your image for it is a caveman-like club, you can imagine the club being broken in half, say. If, instead, the card called is the two of hearts and your normal image of it is a simple farm hen, you might imagine it with an extraordinarily large tail.

The systems described in this chapter are basic to the remembering of cards, and it does not take much to see that a memory system such as this can be of enormous help in the actual playing of card games. You have probably watched people repeating over and over to themselves the cards that they know have been put down or are in other players' hands and you have probably seen them sigh with exasperation at their inability to remember them accurately.

With your new memory system, such tasks will become easy and a joy. Whether you use it for serious card playing or simply for enjoyment, throughout the process you will be exercising your creative memory powers and increasing the usefulness of your brain.

Next, let's take a look at how to remember long numbers in general and mobile and phone numbers in particular.

Raising your IQ by using the long number memory system

You will probably have found the long number memory test you did in Chapter 1 particularly difficult. That is because most people, in IQ tests, cannot remember numbers more than seven or eight digits in length.

Given a long number such as 95862190377 to memorise, most people will try a variety of strategies, including:

- repeating the build-up continually as the number is presented, eventually getting bogged down in the very repetition process itself

- subdividing the number into two- or three-number groups, eventually losing both the order and content of these

- working out mathematical relationships between the numbers as they are presented, inevitably losing track of the original order or the numbers themselves

- picturing the number as it is presented, the picture becoming more and more blurred as the long number is presented in its entirety.

If you think back to your own performance in the initial long number memory test in Chapter 1, you will probably realise that your own approach was one of, or a combination of, these approaches.

Once again, the major system comes to the rescue, making the task of memorising long numbers easy and also enjoyable.

Instead of using the major system as a peg system for remembering lists of 100 and 1000 you take advantage of its flexibility. Going back to the basic code and the initial memory image words you chose for the numbers from 0 to 100, you use the memory image words in conjunction with the link system to remember any long number you like.

Pairing numbers with the major system's memory image words

For example, take the number used at the beginning of this chapter – 95862190377. It is composed, in sequence, of the following smaller numbers, each here followed by their major system memory image word:

95 – Ball   86 – Fish   21 – Net   90 – Base   37 – Mac   7 – Key

In order to remember this almost 'impossibly long' number, all you now have to do is use the basic link system, making the words into a simple and imaginative little story. For example, you could imagine a brilliant, rainbow-coloured *ball* bouncing with a loud 'boing!' off the head of a gigantic and beautifully coloured *fish* that had just fought its way out of a very tangled and dripping-wet *net*, which was slowly collapsing to the *base* level of a pier, where it wrapped itself around a man wearing a fawn-coloured and wind-blown *mac*, just as he was bending over to pick up a *key*, which he had dropped onto the pier with a loud clang.

Now, close your eyes and re-envision this little story.

Next, recalling the memory image words, transform them back into the numbers, and you will get:

b – 9   l – 5   f – 8   sh – 6   n – 2   t – 1   b – 9   s – 0   m – 3
c – 7   k – 7   95862190377

Try it in threes

It is not essential to remember long numbers using groups of only two. It is just as easy, and sometimes even easier, to consider the numbers in subgroups of three. Try this with the number 851429730584. It is composed of:

851 – Fault   429 – Rainbow   730 – Cameos   584 – Lever

In order to remember this number, which is even longer than the previous one, it is once again a matter of using your basic link system to make up a little image story using your basic memory image words. Using your imagination, you can see in your mind some gigantic universal force that could cause a break or a *fault* in beautiful and shimmering *rainbow*-coloured *cameos*, which are so heavy they need a gigantic *lever* to move them.

Once again, close your eyes and show the little image story on your inner screen.

Next, recall the words and, transforming them, you get:

f – 8   l – 5   t – 1   r – 4   n – 2   b – 9   c – 7   m – 3   s – 0
l – 5   v – 8   r – 4   851429730584

Improvise

Another system for remembering long numbers, especially if you have not committed the major system's memory image words to memory, is to improvise with the basic major system memory code, making up four-consonant words from the number you have to remember.

For example, with a 16-digit number, such as 1582907191447620, you could make up the following 4-digit numbers and memory image words:

1582 – telephone   9071 – basket   9144 – botherer   7620 – cushions

For a memorable story you could imagine a red *telephone*, ringing loudly and melodically being thrown in a long and graceful parabolic curve into a *basket*, where an annoying person (a *botherer*) is jammed, bottom down (as in comedy films), while other people are throwing multicoloured *cushions* in all kinds of different materials at him.

Again, close your eyes and imagine the story, then fill in the words and numbers in the space provided.

_____

_____

_____

_____

If you ever run into difficulty with the order of the words, you can resolve this simply by using, instead of the link system, either the number-shape or the number-rhyme system.

For example, using the original number given at the beginning of this chapter – 95862190377 – you would simply link ball to your memory image for the number 1, fish to your key image for the number 2, net to your key image for the number 3.

Using other pegging systems

You could also use both the Roman room system and the alphabet system, simply placing the words you had decoded from the long number either alphabetically or in your Roman room. Decide which approach to the memorisation of long numbers is best for you. Then, to check on the amazing difference this method for number memorisation can make, go back to your original tests at the start of the book and see just how easy those initial numbers are to memorise now.

Some added benefits

Once you have mastered this skill, you will have improved your memory and your creative imagination even further and also actually raised your IQ. One subsection of IQ measurements involves the ability to remember numbers. Between 6 and 7 is the average person's limit; a score of 9 or more puts you, in that subsection of the test, in the IQ range of 150 and more. Just think where your newfound skill will rank you in this section of the IQ tests! The jump from abstract numbers to practical telephone and mobile numbers is but a short one.

The telephone number memory system

Even if you have numbers stored digitally on mobiles, PDAs and other devices, there'll be plenty of occasions when you need to remember phone numbers without them.

Remembering telephone numbers turns out to be easier than forgetting them, and, once again, it is the major system that comes to the rescue in this situation.

Most telephone numbers find themselves stored on mobile phones and PDAs or else written on scraps of paper in a limitless range of sizes, colours and shapes, in pockets, drawers, briefcases – in fact, anywhere and on anything you care to mention: that is, everywhere but the key place they should be – in your memory.

How to remember telephone numbers

To remember telephone numbers you need to 'translate' each digit of the number you have to remember into a letter from the basic code for the major system. Using the letters you have transcribed, make up catchy words and phrases that link you back to both the number and the person.

For example, start with the ten people whose numbers you tried to remember in the initial telephone number test you took in Chapter 1.

Name	Number
Healthfood shop	787-5953
Tennis partner	640-7336
Weather bureau	691-0262
Newsagent	242-9111
Florist	725-8397
Garage	781-3702
Theatre	869-9521
Nightclub	644-1616
Community centre	457-8910
Restaurant	354-6350

The following examples are possible ways to remember these ten telephone numbers.

- **Healthfood shop: 787-5953** This translates into the letters 'g f g-l b l m'. Your memory phrase, starting with each of the numbers' letters, could be 'Good Food Guides: heaLthy.Body heaLthy Mind'. In your imagination you could visualise healthy owners of the shop, and the Greek ideal of *mens sana in corpore sano*, perhaps even visualising an Olympic Games in which all the participants buy their food from this healthfood shop.

- **Tennis partner: 640-7336** This translates into the letters 'sh r s-c m m sh'. Your visual memory phrase here might be: 'Shows Real Skill – Can Make Masterly SHots'. Again, you could visualise your tennis partner making the statement come true.

- **Weather bureau: 691-0262** This translates into the letters 'sh p d-s n sh n'. Here, you could imagine yourself as a sculptor of the sun, making it into various shapes and, therefore, yourself as a god of meteorology, and use a very condensed phrase that includes only the letters that translate back into the number: 'SHaPeD SuNSHiNe'!

- **Newsagent: 242-9111** This translates into the letters 'n r n-p d t d'. Again, you can use the condensing technique, imagining the newsagent shouting: 'News! Read News! – uPDaTeD!'

- **Florist: 725-8397** This translates into the letters 'g n l-f m b g'. Imagine yourself just having given a bouquet of beautiful flowers to the one you love and wanting to shout about it to the world: 'Good News Lovers! Flowers Make Beautiful Gifts!'

- **Garage: 781-3702** This translates into the letters 'c f t-m g s n'. Imagine the garage as super-efficient, turning around every car within a day and giving them back to their owners in a condition as perfect as when they came off the assembly line: 'Cars Fixed Today! Made Good aS New'.

- **Theatre: 869-9521** This translates into the letters 'f sh p-p l n t'. Imagine that your local theatre is putting on a number of plays by Shakespeare and that, as you attend each of them, you experience the entire gamut of emotions: 'Finest SHakespearian Productions Produce Laughter aNd Tears'.

- **Nightclub: 644-1616** This translates into the letters 'ch r r-d j d j'. The latter part, rather conveniently can stay as it is. All you have to do for this particular number is find a little phrase for the first three letters: 'CHanges Revolving Records – DJ! DJ!'

- **Community centre: 457-8910** This translates into the letters 'r l c-f b d s'. Imagine the whole joint jumping: 'Really Lively Community – Football! Badminton! Dances! Swimming!'

- **Restaurant: 354-6350** This translates into the letters 'm l r-ch m l s'. Imagine the restaurant offering excellent cuisine at reasonable prices: 'My Lovely Restaurant – CHarges Moderate; Luscious Selections'.

Solutions for difficult telephone numbers

In some cases, the combination of numbers may present a greater than usual level of difficulty, making it seem almost impossible to devise appropriate phrases or words for them. The solutions are still fairly simple, however. You can make up inappropriate words out of the numbers you have to deal with, then use the basic system, making absurd and exaggerated images to link with the person whose telephone number you are trying to remember.

For example, if the telephone number of one of your friends, whose hobby is golf, is 491-4276, you would take the major system memory image words for 49 (rap), 142 (drain) and 76 (cage). Your image for remembering this number could be of your friend rapping loudly on a *drain*, which has bars like a *cage*, with his golf club.

These examples are, of course, very particular. It is now up to you to apply the system outlined to the telephone numbers that you need to remember.

Over to you

Now that you have mastered the basics of the telephone number memory system, it is essential that you associate and link it to your own life. Therefore, in the space provided below, make a note of the names and telephone numbers of at least ten people or places you need to remember and, before reading the next chapter, make sure that you have your own ten numbers firmly pictured in your memory.

As you form the images, remember the 12 memory techniques, realising that the more enjoyable, humorous and imaginative you make them, the better your memory for those numbers will be.

My ten most important telephone numbers

1 _____

2 _____

3 _____

4 _____

5 _____

6 _____

7 _____

8 _____

9 _____

10 _____

Let's next turn to another facet of life that throws up details people often find hard to remember – schedules and diary dates.

Memory system for schedules and appointments

In this chapter, two systems are introduced, the first of which is for immediate daily use, the second for remembering schedules and appointments for an entire week.

As with telephone numbers, many people find appointments and schedules hard to remember. They use similar systems for coping with this, the commonest of which, of course, is the diary or, these days, a PDA or computer desk diary tool. Unfortunately, many people don't always keep their diaries with them or can access their computers when they need them.

Pegging your daily schedule

The first memory system I want to introduce you to uses the basic peg system.

Simply link the number in your system with the hour of your appointment. As there are 24 hours in a day, you can either join shorter systems together, to make an appropriate total of 24, or use the first 24 peg words in one of the larger systems.

Assume that you have the following appointments:

7 Early-morning run/gym workout   10 Dentist   1 Lunch
6 Board meeting   10 Late film

At the beginning of the day, you run through the list and check for words that have associations.

The time for your early-morning run or gym workout is 7.00 a.m., represented by the major system memory image word (key) for the number 7. Imagine yourself or all the people at the gym physically unlocking the door to super health with a big *key*.

At 10.00 a.m. (daze), you have a dentist's appointment. Imagine him putting earphones on your head that play such soothing music you are literally in a *daze*, unable to feel any pain. (What is interesting about this example is the fact that if you imagine this particular situation, in reality you may actually be able to reduce the pain!)

Your next appointment, at 1.00 p.m. (translate this as 13, for 13:00 hours), is for lunch. The memory image word for 13 is 'dam'. Imagine your table and then your guests and yourself, sitting down for lunch at the top of an enormous *dam*, looking at the limpid lake on one side and the roaring waterfall on the other.

At 6.00 p.m. you have a board meeting. The major system memory image word for 18 (18:00 hours) is 'Daffy'. The association here is clear and memorable: imagine the confidential matters of your board meeting being discussed with Daffy Duck presiding!

Finally, you have an appointment at 10.00 p.m. (22:00 hours) to see a late film. The major system memory word for 22 is 'nan', so you can imagine going to the film with your grandmother or, if you like Indian food, imagine yourself eating the Indian bread (nan) throughout the film. You can easily 'order' these five appointments by either using the link system to link the images you have just created in order or simply placing each of the five images on your basic number-shape or number-rhyme system.

Timetabling your weekly schedule

The second system for remembering schedules and appointments can be used for an entire week.

Take Sunday as day 1 of the week and ascribe a number to each of the other days:

Sunday	1
Monday	2
Tuesday	3
Wednesday	4
Thursday	5
Friday	6
Saturday	7

Having given a number to each day, treat the hours as we did in the first system discussed above and as they appear in railway and airline timetables – that is, using the 24-hour clock. Each day has 24 hours, from 24:00 (midnight) to 1.00 a.m. (01:00), noon (12:00), 1.00 p.m. (13:00) and back to midnight again (24:00). Thus, for any hour and day of the week a two- or three-digit number can be formed – day first, hour second. All that is then necessary is to translate the number into the word of a major system list. Having arrived at the word, you link it with the appropriate appointment.

For example, suppose you had an appointment to view a car you wanted to buy at 9.00 a.m. on Tuesday. Tuesday is represented by the number 3, which, in the major system, translates into the letter 'm'. The hour, 9, translates into the letters 'b, p'. Referring to the basic list, you will see that the memory image word for Tuesday at 9.00 a.m. (39) is 'map'. To remember this appointment, then, you might imagine the car you are going to see as bursting through a giant map, wrapped in a giant map or driving across a giant map.

As another example, imagine you have an appointment for a guitar lesson at 5.00 p.m. (hour number 17) on a Thursday (day number 5). The number Thursday at 5.00 p.m. translates into is 517, the word from the list for this being 'leading'. To remember this, imagine yourself leading an entire orchestra with your solo guitar. Use the SMASHIN' SCOPE' memory techniques and imagine that you can hear all the sounds, feel your guitar and see the audience.

Simplifying the system

This system does require a fairly thorough knowledge of the larger numbers in the major system. This can be made easier by 'rotating' the hours of the day to suit the times when you have most of your appointments. If your day does not usually start until 10.00 a.m., then 10.00 a.m. can be considered number 1 in your appointment memory system. In this manner, the most important and often-used hours in your day will nearly always be represented by only two-digit numbers – that is, the numbers from 10 to 100 in the major system. As with the technique for remembering your daily schedule, you can 'order' your week's schedule by attaching the images, in order, to the major system.

For practical purposes, it is usually best to start with the system for your daily schedule, becoming skilled and familiar with it before moving on to the system for your weekly schedule.

Now we are going to apply the memory system to enable you to recall, with ease, historic dates as well as those birthdays and anniversaries everyone forgets!

Memory system for important historical dates

The system you are about to learn will assist you in the memorisation of significant dates in history.

One of the memory tests you completed in Chapter 1 was on a list of ten such dates. They were:

1 1666   Great Fire of London

2 1770   Beethoven's birthday

3 1215   Signing of Magna Carta

4 1917   Russian Revolution

5 1454   First printing press

6 1815   Battle of Waterloo

7 1608   Invention of the telescope

8 1905   Einstein's Theory of Relativity

9 1789   French Revolution

10 1776   American Declaration of Independence

The method you can use to remember these or any other such dates is simple – it is similar to the method for remembering telephone numbers.

All you have to do is make a word or string of words from the letters that represent the numbers of the date. In most cases, there is no point in including the 1, representing the thousand, as you know the approximate date in any case. Let us try this system on the dates given above.

1 The Great Fire of London in 1666 practically destroyed the city, leaving it a heap of ashes. Our memory phrase for the date 1666 would thus be, 'aSHes, aSHes, aSHes!' or 'CHarred aSHes Generally'.

2 Beethoven is famous for many musical accomplishments, and perhaps his greatest achievement was the Ninth Symphony, which included a choir. His style of music made full use of the percussion instruments. Knowing this, remembering his birthday in 1770 becomes easy: 'Crashing CHoral Symphony'.

3 The signing of the Magna Carta in 1215 marked a new age of sense and reason. To remember this date, we can use the phrase 'New Document – Liberalisation'.

4 The Russian Revolution of 1917 was an uprising of the people against what they considered oppression. They demanded greater equality in the form of communism. Our memory phrase could be, 'People Demand Communism'.

5 Printing presses are often great rotating machines that churn out thousands of pages a minute. We can imagine a small version of this as the first printing press, in 1454, which could be remembered by the word 'RoLleR'.

6 The Battle of Waterloo in 1815 was a triumph for Wellington, but can be considered fatal for Napoleon. Once again, we can use a memory word rather than a memory phrase to remember the date: 'FaTaL'.

7 The invention of the telescope by Hans Lippershey in 1608 changed the way in which man saw the sky. Our memory phrase, therefore, could be, 'CHanged Sky Focus'.

8 In 1905, Einstein's Theory of Relativity shed new light on the way in which matter and energy exist. His theory solved a number of puzzles that had occupied great minds, but also gave rise to many more. Our image memory word for this could therefore be PuZZLe.

9 During the French Revolution in 1789, the king was ranged against the people. Hence, we can remember the date by means of the phrase, 'King Fights People'.

10 The American Declaration of Independence in 1776 marked a feeling of optimism and confidence in a new way of life in America. This can be encapsulated in one word: 'CoCKSure'.

In the next chapter we'll apply a memory system to remembering birthdays and anniversaries, so we never have those embarrassing memory lapses again.

Remembering birthdays, anniversaries and days

This next system will be easy for you because it makes use of systems you have already learned. It is also easier than most other systems suggested for remembering such items because the large memory system you have learned – the major system – can be used as a 'key' for the months and days (other systems usually require codenames that have to be especially devised for the months).

How the system works

The months are assigned the numbers 1 to 12 and given the appropriate memory image word for the major system.

1	January	Day
2	February	Noah
3	March	Ma
4	April	Ra
5	May	Law
6	June	Jaw
7	July	Key
8	August	Fee
9	September	Bay
10	October	Daze
11	November	Dad
12	December	Dan

To remember a birthday, anniversary or historical date, all that you need to do is form an image that links the month and day words and the date you wish to remember. For example, if your friend's birthday falls on 15 June, the memory image word from the major system for 6, and therefore June, is 'jaw' and for 15 is 'dale'. To link them, imagine spending a deliriously happy day with your friend in a beautiful dale and your big 'jaws', responding to your state of bliss, grin from ear to ear!

Say you wanted to remember your parents' wedding anniversary and it falls on 25 February. The memory image word for 2, and therefore, February is 'Noah'; and for 25 is 'nail'. Imagine Noah, who paired up the animals, trying to marry your parents by nailing their marriage vows to the ark!

Historical dates can become just as easy to remember. For example, the date when the United Nations came into formal existence was 24 October. The major system memory image word for 10, and October, therefore is 'daze'; and for 24 is 'Nero'. Imagine a horse, dazed from the blaze caused by Nero's burning city, running into a situation where there is no strife.

The memory system outlined in this chapter can be linked effectively with the previous system for remembering historical dates by year. By doing this, you will provide yourself with a *complete* system for remembering dates.

Let's take a look next at ways in which we can remember essential vocabulary and the 100 basic words that make up 50 per cent of all conversation.

Memory systems for vocabulary and language

Vocabulary is the basic building block of language, it is desirable and necessary to develop methods that will help you to learn and remember words more easily.

Vocabulary is the most important single factor in the development of efficient reading and also academic and business success.

One of the better ways to remember words is to learn the prefixes (letters, syllables or words recurring before root words), the suffixes (letters, syllables or words recurring at the end of root words) and the roots (words from which other words are derived) that occur most frequently in the language you are attempting to learn. A comprehensive list of these appears in the vocabulary chapters of *The Speed Reading Book*.

Improving your word memory – general tips

Here are some more tips for how to improve your word memory.

1 Browse through a good dictionary, studying the ways in which the prefixes, suffixes and roots of the language are used. Whenever possible, use association to strengthen your recall.

2 Introduce a fixed number of new words into your vocabulary every day. New words are retained only if the principle of repetition, as explained earlier, is practised. Use your new words in context and as many times as possible after you have initially learned them.

3 Consciously look for new words in the language. This directing of your attention, known as mental set, leaves the 'hooks' of your memory more open to catching new linguistic fish!

These are general learning aids that will assist your memory when acquiring knowledge of a language. They may be applied to English, as a means of improving your present vocabulary, or to any foreign languages you are beginning to learn.

Having established a general foundation for learning words, let us be more specific about how to remember particular words.

Improving your word memory – specifics

As with other memory systems, the key word is *association*. In the context of language learning, it is well to associate sounds, images and similarities using the fact that certain languages are grouped in 'families' and have related words.

To give you an idea of this linking method, let's consider a few words from English, French, Latin and German. In English, let's say that you want to remember the word 'vertigo', which means dizziness or giddiness, a sense of whirling and loss of balance when looking down from a height or as a result of an inner-ear infection. To imprint this word on your memory you can associate the sound of it with the phrase 'Where to go?' which is the kind of question you might ask if you felt that the world was whirling about you.

Two words that many people confuse in the English language are 'acrophobia', which is a morbid fear of heights, and 'agoraphobia', a morbid fear of open spaces. The distinction can be firmly established if you associate the 'acro' in 'acrophobia' with 'acrobat' (a person who performs at a great height) and the 'agora' in 'agoraphobia' with 'agriculture', bringing to mind images of open fields.

Foreign languages are more approachable when one realises that they form groups. Practically all European languages (with the exception of Finnish, Hungarian and Basque) are part of the Indo-European group and, consequently, contain a number of words that are similar in both sound and meaning. For example, consider the words for 'father': German, 'Vater'; Latin, 'pater'; French, 'père'; Italian and Spanish, 'padre'.

A knowledge of Latin is of enormous help in understanding all the Romance languages, in which many of the words are similar. The Latin word for love is 'amor'. Related to 'love' in the English language is the word 'amorous', which means 'inclined to love; in love; and of, or pertaining to, love'. The links are obvious. Similarly, the Latin word for 'God' is 'Deus'. In English, the words 'deity' and 'deify' mean, respectively, 'divine status; a god; the Creator' and 'to make a god of'. French was derived from the speech of the Roman legionnaires, who called the head 'testa', hence 'tête'. About 50 per cent of ordinary English speech is derived from Latin (plus Greek), either directly or by way of Norman French, leading to many direct similarities between French and English.

In addition to similarities based on such language groupings, foreign words can be remembered in a manner not unlike that explained for remembering English words. As we are discussing French, the following two examples are appropriate. In French, the word for book is 'livre'. This can be remembered more readily if you think of the first four letters of the word 'library', which is a place where books are classified and studied. The French word for 'pen' is 'plume', which in English refers to a bird's feather, especially a large one used for ornament. This immediately brings to mind the quill pens used widely before the invention of the steel nib, fountain pen and ballpoint pen. The links in the chain – plume – feather – quill – pen – make remembering the French word for a 'pen' a simple task.

Apart from Latin, Greek and French, the rest of English is largely Anglo-Saxon, and German. This has given rise to countless words that are the same in German and English – will, hand, arm, bank, halt, and wolf – whereas others are closely related – light (Licht), night (Nacht), book (Buch), stick (Stock), ship (Schiff), house (Haus).

Learning languages, then, both our own and those of other countries, need not be the frustrating and depressing experience it so often is. It is simply a matter of organising the information you want to learn in such a way as to enable your memory to 'hook on' to every available scrap of information – and it can!

The 100 basic words that make up 50 per cent of all conversation

One way to get a head start in learning is to realise that, in most languages, 50 per cent of all conversation is made up of only 100 words. If you apply the major system to the memorisation of these you are already 50 per cent of the way towards being able to understand the basic conversation of any native speaker.

To help you along, the 100 basic words in the English language are listed below. You will find that if you compare them with their counterparts in, say, French, German, Swedish, Italian, Spanish, Portuguese, Russian, Chinese, Japanese and Esperanto, nearly 50 per cent of them are almost the same as the English words, with only minor variations in the accent and stress of the words.

1	a, an	20	from	37	little	55	or
2	after	21	to go	38	love	56	other
3	again		(I go)		(I love)	57	our
4	all	22	good	39	make	58	out
5	almost	23	goodbye		(I make)	59	over
6	also	24	happy	40	many	60	people
7	always	25	have	41	me	61	place
8	and		(I have)	42	more	62	please
9	because	26	he	43	most	63	same
10	before	27	hello	44	much	64	see (I see)
11	big	28	here	45	my	65	she
12	but	29	how	46	new	66	so
13	can (I can)	30	I	47	no	67	some
14	come	31	I am	48	not	68	sometimes
	(I come)	32	if	49	now	69	still
15	either/or	33	in	50	of	70	such
16	find (I find)	34	know	51	often	71	tell (I tell)
17	first		(I know)	52	on	72	thank you
18	for	35	last	53	one	73	that
19	friend	36	like (I like)	54	only	74	the

75	their	81	think	87	us	94	which
76	them		(I think)	88	use (I use)	95	who
77	then	82	this	89	very	96	why
78	there is,	83	time	90	we	97	with
	there are	84	to	91	what	98	yes
79	they	85	under	92	when	99	you
80	thing	86	up	93	where	100	your

By applying the 12 memory techniques to the memorisation of these words and others, you will find that language learning can be the easy, enjoyable task that most children find it to be. Adults can learn languages as well as children. Children simply open their minds more to the language and are not afraid to make mistakes. They repeat and make associations with the basics, listen more attentively, copy and mimic and generally have a thoroughly good time without as much instruction as we adults think we need.

The following chapters show how to apply our memory techniques to the much-requested area of how to remember which name goes with which face, recalling a 'forgotten' item, place and number, revising for examinations, memorising speeches, jokes, poems and books and 'catching' those elusive dreams.

Remembering names and faces

Remembering names and faces is one of the most important aspects of our lives, and people can find it tricky.

The reason for the difficulty lies in the fact that, in most instances, the names have no real 'connection' to the faces. In earlier ages it was exactly the opposite – the whole system that developed for giving people names was based on memory and association. The man you regularly saw covered in white flour with dough all over his hands was Mr Baker, the man you regularly saw in his own and everyone else's gardens was Mr Gardener and the man who laboured all day over a hot fire pounding metal was Mr Blacksmith. Names were based on helping you make the image association with the person: when young Miss Farmer went to the city, there was no longer any association between her and her name. Therefore you would forget her name unless you could create a new appropriate association. As the generations changed and the family name became more and more removed from its original meaning, the task of the memorisation of names and faces became increasingly difficult, reaching the current situation in which the name is a word that has no immediate associations with the face.

There are two major methods that you can use to memorise names and faces, each supporting the other. The first is my 'social etiquette' method; the second is the 'mnemonic' method.

The 'social etiquette' method

Here's a method for remembering names and faces that guarantees you will never again find yourself in a situation where you are introduced rapidly to five people and hurriedly repeat, 'Pleased to meet you, pleased to meet you, pleased to meet you, pleased to meet you, pleased to meet you', having, in reality, been introduced to only the five pairs of shoes at which you stared in embarrassment because you know you are immediately going to forget all the names anyway (which you do!).

My method requires just two simple things of you:

1 an interest in the people you meet

2 politeness.

The method is called the 'social etiquette' method because it is the same as one that you might find described in a book of etiquette. Even writers of etiquette books, however, often fail to realise that the original rules were made not simply to enforce codes of conduct but to allow people to interact on a friendly basis. The rules being structured formally only to enable the people to meet and remember one another.

Select from the following steps those that will help you the most.

1 **Mental set**
   Before you enter a situation in which you will meet people, mentally prepare yourself to succeed. Many people enter such situations 'knowing' that they have a bad memory for names and faces and consequently set about proving it to themselves. If you 'know' that your memory is going to improve, you will notice an immediate improvement. When preparing yourself for meeting people, therefore, try to make sure that you are as poised and relaxed as possible and, wherever feasible, give yourself a two- to five-minute break to prepare.

2 **Observe**
   When you are meeting people, make sure that you look them straight in the eye. Don't shuffle around, with your eyes on the floor or looking into the distance. As you look at someone's face, be aware of his or her special facial characteristics, for this

will help you also with the 'second mnemonic' approach to the memorisation of names and faces. Make sure that you follow a 'guided tour', from the top of the head to the tip of the chin (see page 164), enumerating the various characteristics and the ways in which they can be classified and typified. The more you become skilled at the art of observation, the more you will realise just how different one face is from another. If you can sharpen your observational powers, you will have made a giant step towards improving your memory.

Blank looking, instead of real seeing, is one the major causes of poor memory. You can prepare your mind for this kind of seeing by 'exercising' your observational powers in public places. At different times, give yourself different parts of the face to look at, so that on one day you might concentrate on noses, another day on eyebrows, another day on ears and another on general head shapes. You will find to your surprise that each part of each face varies enormously from person to person and that your increasing observation of such differences will help you to remember the new faces that you meet.

3 Listen
Consciously listen, paying attention as much as you possibly can to the sound of the name of the person to whom you are being introduced. This is a crucial stage of the introductory process, at which point many people fail because they concentrate more on the fact that they are going to forget than on the sound of the name of the person to whom they are being introduced!

4 Request repetition
Even if you have heard the name fairly well, politely say something in the order of, 'I'm sorry, would you mind repeating the name?' Repetition is an important memory aid – each repetition of any item you wish to learn greatly increases the probability of your remembering it.

5 Verify the pronunciation
Once you have been given a person's name, immediately confirm, by asking the person to whom the name belongs, if you

have the correct pronunciation. This confirms your interest and once again repeats the name, increasing the probability of your remembering it.

6 Request the spelling
If there is any doubt about the spelling of the person's name, politely or playfully ask for the spelling. This again confirms your interest and allows you another natural repetition of the name.

7 Your new hobby – derivations
With a natural enthusiasm, explain that one of your new hobbies is the background and derivation of names and then politely ask the person to whom you have been introduced if he or she knows anything about the history of his or her family name. (Be sure you know the history of your own surname – something that is becoming increasingly easier to do with the increasing availability of online family tree sites due to the rise in popularity of this hobby.) More and more people not only know at least some part of the background of their family's name but also are enthusiastic about discussing it. Once again, you will have confirmed your interest in the person, as well as having created an opportunity for more repetition of his or her name.

8 Exchange cards
The Japanese and Chinese, particularly, have developed the exchange of cards into a major social function, realising how useful it is for memory. If you are really interested in remembering people's names, make sure that you have a very presentable card to give them, then, in most cases, they will give you their own or write their details down for you.

9 Repetition in conversation
Carrying the principles of interest, politeness and repetition further, make sure that during conversations with people newly met, you repeat their names wherever possible. This repetition helps to implant the name more firmly in your memory and it is also socially more rewarding, for it involves the other person more intimately in the conversation. It is far more satisfying for them to hear you say, 'Yes, as Mary has just said …' than to hear you say, 'Yes, as she [as you point] has just said …'

10 Repeat internally

During any little pause in the conversation, look analytically and with interest at the various people who are speaking and about whom others are speaking, repeating internally to yourself their names, which by now will be becoming second nature to you.

11 Check during longer breaks

If you have gone to get a drink for someone or for yourself, or for any other reason are momentarily alone in a crowd, spend the time scanning everyone you have met, repeating to yourself their names, the spellings of their names, any background material you have gathered about their names, plus any other items of interest that have arisen during the conversation. In this way, you will be surrounding each name with associations, thus building up a mapped network in your own mind that will increase the probability of your recalling them in the future. You will be positively using the process described in the next chapter.

12 Repetition at parting

As you say farewell, make sure you use the name of the person to whom you are saying it. Thus, by this time you will have used both the primacy and recency time aspects of memory, as outlined in Chapter 2, having consolidated both your initial and final moments during the learning period.

13 Reviews

When you have parted from the new people, quickly flash through your mind all their names and faces. Alternatively, when possible (for example, at a party), get photographs (either the formal ones or informal ones) of the event.

14 The reversal principle

Wherever possible, reverse the processes through which you have just been. For example, when you are being introduced to someone else for the first time, repeat your own name, give the spelling of it, and, if it seems appropriate, even give the derivation or background. Similarly, make sure you present, where appropriate, your personal card. Throughout conversations, if you are referring to yourself, use your own name. This will help others to remember you, as well as encouraging them to use their names rather than pronouns to help you remember them, too. In addition to being more polite, this approach will make the entire conversation more personal, enjoyable and friendly.

15 Pace yourself

There is a tendency, because of the stress of the initial meeting situation, to rush through it. The great names-and-faces memorisers and founders of social etiquette invariably take their time, making sure that they have said at least one personal thing to everyone they meet. The Queen of England is a good example in this regard.

16 Have fun

If you make the learning of names and faces a serious and enjoyable game, the right side of your brain will feel far freer and more open to making the imaginative associations and connections necessary for good memory. Children have 'better memories' for names and faces than adults because their minds are superior and simply because they naturally apply all the techniques outlined in The Memory Book.

17 The 'plus one' principle

If you would normally remember only between 2 and 5 of 30 people you have newly met, as the average person would, give yourself the goal of remembering just 1 more person. This establishes in your mind the principle of success and does not place the unnecessary stress of trying to remember everyone first time out. Apply the plus one principle each time you are in a new situation and your road to success in the memorisation of names and faces is guaranteed. A useful exercise or game at this stage is to take the first letter of each of the 17 steps outlined above and make a memorable acronym from them. Use all the SMASHIN' SCOPE principles.

The mnemonic names and faces memory method

The mnemonic method for remembering names and faces uses exactly the same techniques as those outlined in Chapter 3, emphasising imagination and association.

The steps are as follows.

1 Make sure that you have a clear mental image of the name of the person you want to remember.

2 Make sure you can actually 'hear again' the sound of the person's name.

3 Very carefully examine the face of the person you have been introduced to, noting in detail the characteristics outlined below.

4 Look for facial characteristics that are unusual, extraordinary or unique.

5 Mentally reconstruct the person's face, using your imagination in the way that a cartoonist does to exaggerate any noteworthy features.

6 Associate – using your imagination, exaggeration and the 12 general memory techniques – any outstanding features with the name of the person.

The quickest and easiest way for you to learn how to apply these steps is to put them immediately into practice.

Below are 20 faces and names on which you will be tested (double the original test on pages 15 to 17).

1 Mr Mogambi   2 Mr Knorr

3 Ms Woodrowe

4 Mr Kokowski

5 Mrs Volkein

6 Mr Cliffe

7 Mr Momatt

8 Miss Ashton

9 Mr Mapley

10 Mr Dewhurst

11 Ms Jabanardi

12 Mr Suzuki

13 Mr Welsh

14 Mr Macinnes

15 Ms Knight

16 Ms Parsons

17 Ms Cook

18 Mr Pang

19 Mr Burn

20 Ms Hammond

Suggestions are given below and on page 166 on how you might apply the steps to remembering the names associated with 5 of these faces. Look carefully at them and at the remaining 15, creating your own links to remember as many as you can, then test yourself by filling in their names at the end of the chapter.

Memorising faces

If you wanted, for example, to remember the names of the faces shown here, you would simply apply the techniques outlined, looking closely at the faces to find some characteristics that you could imaginatively associate with the name, then make your mnemonic image. For example, Mr Mapley (No. 9) is easy to remember as his face is deeply furrowed and lined, like a map – the image is thus a map leading to Mapley. Similarly, Mr Suzuki (No. 12) has particularly pronounced eyebrows, which you could imagine as the flamboyant handlebars of a Suzuki motorbike. Ms Knight (No. 15) has long, flowing hair that hangs, so you might imagine her bending her head down at the top of a castle, with some valiant knight climbing up her tresses to rescue her. Mr Burn (No. 19) has very closely cropped and dark hair. You might imagine that his face is the countryside and his hair is the result of a gigantic bush or forest fire that has burned all the vegetation.

Short-term tip

One other point about remembering people: if you are certain that you will be meeting a person only once and so are not concerned about committing his or her name and face to your long-term memory, it is often useful to use an outstanding item of clothing that the person might be wearing to remember him or her that day. This method, of course, is no good for creating a long-term memory as the person will probably not be wearing the same clothes next time. The same point applies to hairstyles and beards.

Head and facial characteristics

Head

You will usually first meet a person face-to-face, so, before dealing with the rundown of other characteristics, we will first consider the head as a whole.

Look for the general shape of the entire bone structure. You will find that this can be large, medium or small. Within these three categories the following shapes can be found: square, rectangular, round, oval, triangular (with the base at the chin and the point at the scalp), triangular (with the base at the scalp and the point at the chin), broad, narrow, big-boned, or fine-boned.

Fairly early in your meeting, you may see the head from the side and will be surprised at how many different shapes heads can take when seen from this angle. They can be square, rectangular, oval, broad, narrow, round, flat at the front, flat on top, flat at the back, domed at the back, face angled with a jutting chin and slanted forehead or face angled with a receding chin and prominent forehead.

Hair

In earlier days, when hairstyles used to be more consistent and long-lasting, hair served as a better memory hook than it does now. The advent of dyes, sprays, wigs and almost infinitely varied styles makes identification by means of this feature a tricky business. Some of the more basic characteristics, however, can be listed as follows. Men can have thick, fine, wavy, straight, parted, receding, bald, cropped, medium, long, frizzy, a particular colour or they can be bald. Women can have thick, thin, or fine hair. Because of the variability in women's hair it is not advisable to try to remember them by this characteristic alone.

Forehead

Foreheads can generally be divided into the following categories: high, wide, narrow between hairline and eyebrows, narrow from temple to temple, smooth, lined horizontally or lined vertically.

Eyebrows

Eyebrows can be thick, thin, long, short, meeting in the middle, spaced apart, flat, arched, winged, bushy or tapered.

Eyelashes

These can be thick, thin, long, short, curled or straight.

Eyes

People can have large, small, protruding, deep-set, close together, spaced apart, slanted outwards, slanted inwards or unusually coloured eyes, with the entire circle of the iris visible or partially covered by the upper and/or lower lids. Attention may also be paid in some cases to the lid above and the bag below the eye, both of which can be large or small, smooth or wrinkled, puffy or firm.

Nose

When seen from the front, noses can be large, small, narrow, medium, wide, or crooked. When seen from the side, they can be straight, flat, pointed, blunt, snub or upturned, Roman or aquiline, Greek (forming a straight line with the forehead) or concave (caved in).

The base of the nose can also vary considerably in relation to the nostrils, being lower, level or a little higher. The nostrils themselves can also vary be a variety of shapes – straight, curved down, flaring, wide or narrow.

Cheekbones

Cheekbones are often linked very closely with the characteristics of a face when seen front-on. The following three characteristics are often worth noting: are the cheekbones high, prominent or obscured?

Ears

Ears are a part of the face to which few people pay attention to, yet their individuality can be more noteworthy than any other feature. They may be large, small, gnarled, smooth, round, oblong, triangular, flat against the head, protruding, hairy, large lobed, have no lobes or be uneven.

This part of the face is often more appropriate as a memory hook for men than for women, because the latter often have hairstyles that cover their ears.

Lips

People can have a long upper lip, short upper lip or small, thick (bee-stung), wide, thin, upturned, downturned, Cupid's bow, well-shaped or ill-defined lips.

Chin

When seen straight-on, the chin may be long, short, pointed, square, round, double (or multiple), cleft or dimpled. When seen from the side, it can be jutting, straight, double (or multiple) or receding.

Skin

There are all kinds of skin – from smooth, rough, dark, fair, blemished or marked in some way to oily, dry, blotchy, doughy, wrinkled, furrowed, coloured, tattooed, tanned.

Other features

When it comes to men, you can also include the various and varied patterns of facial hair, which range from short sideburns to the full-blooded and face-concealing beard with moustache. There is no point in listing all the variations, and like hairstyles and colours, they can change overnight.

A basic image list

As you establish your names and faces memory techniques, it is useful to have a 'basic image list' for common names you are likely to come across.

In your basic image list, simply have some standard images for such names that you can immediately link to the outstanding facial characteristics of those who have those names. Following is a list of examples of names and images to illustrate how this is done.

- **Ashcroft** the smouldering roof of a burned-out farm building with masses of flaky grey ash.

- **Blake** a gigantic, limpid blue lake in the shape of the letter B.

- **Delaney** a giant ripping out country lanes (de-lane-ing).

- **Evans** vans shaped like the capital letter 'E', the spine of the letter being the top of the van.

- **Farren** a tiny little bird (wren) seen from a long way away.

- **Goddard** God with a 'hard' expression on his face.

- **Humphrey** a delighted prisoner humming a happy song as he is let out from behind the bars.

- **Ivy** ivy.

- **King** a throne.

- **Lawrence** of Arabia!

- **Mercer** someone pleading for and being given mercy.

- **Nunn** nun.

- **Ovett** a veterinary surgeon swinging in a gigantic letter 'O'.

- **Patterson** the pitter-patter of your own child or that of a friend as those little feet scurry across the floor.

- **Quarry** a gigantic open cast mining area showing a strongly coloured ore.

- **Richardson** the son of a 'rich, hard' father.

- **Scott** a kilt, haggis or anything typical, of a Scottish person.

- **Taylor** a suit.

- **Underwood** wood under which you place the image of the person, such as an old, gigantic fallen tree.

- **Villars** a magnificent gleaming white Mediterranean villa.

- **Wade** a person or animal wading thigh-high through a lake.

- **Xanthou** 'Thank you'.

- **Young** a springtime image.

- **Zimmermann** someone 'zimming' (made up word for skimming/zooming) across the surface of water.

16 _____ 6 _____

12 _____ 9 _____

19 _____

4 _____

15 _____

11 _____

18 _____

10 _____

3 _____

8 _____

14 _____

17 _____

7 _____

5 _____

The Memory Book

2 _____   1 _____

20 _____   13 _____

Before we explore the ultimate memory system in Part 4, in the next chapter let's follow a simple way to remember those elusive dreams we invariably forget as we wake up.

Catching your dreams

The ability to remember dreams may appear to vary enormously from individual to individual and you will be pleased to read that everyone with the memory techniques you have already learned can tap into their subconscious minds.

Some people have such bad memories for their dreams that they sincerely believe they do not dream at all. This is not the case, as research carried out during the past 20 years has shown that every human being has regular periods throughout the night when dreaming takes place. This is evidenced by periods of REM sleep – REM standing for 'rapid eye movement' – when the eyelids flicker and flutter and occasionally the entire body twitches as the body internally 'sees' and 'moves' with the imaginary story. If you have a cat or a dog, you may have noticed this kind of activity while it sleeps, for most higher mammals also dream.

How to memorise your dreams

The first step in the memorisation of your dreams is the actual retrieval of the dream itself. This you can accomplish by 'setting' your mind just before you go to sleep. As you begin to drift off, gently and firmly repeat to yourself, 'I am a dream rememberer, I am a dream rememberer, I am a dream rememberer.' This will programme your brain when you wake up to give priority to recalling your dreams. It may take as many as three weeks before you 'catch' your first one, but the process is infallible.

Once you have caught a dream, you enter the second stage of dream memorisation. That is a tricky and 'dangerous' moment, for if you become too excited by the fact that you have actually caught one, you will lose it! That is because, for this type of memorisation, your brain needs to remain, for a while, in a *non-excited* state. You must learn to maintain an almost meditational calm, gently reviewing the main elements of the dream. You then very gently select two or three of the main images from the dream and attach these, using the memory techniques you have learned (which are dreamlike in themselves) to one of your basic peg or link systems.

Let's imagine, for example, that you have dreamed you were an Inuit stranded on an ice-floe at the North Pole and you are writing, messages calling for help in the Northern sky with gigantic felt-tipped pens, forming multicoloured words that look like the aurora borealis. For this you would need only two items from any peg system.

Take, for this example, the alphabet system (outlined on page 83). For this you would imagine that, on the ice-floe with you, is a gigantic, and hairy *ape*, shivering exaggeratedly in the cold with you and thumping his chest to keep warm as an enormous *bee* buzzes in and out of the multicoloured images you are writing in the sky.

Note that, although the alphabet system image word for the letter 'A' suggested in Chapter 8 is '*ace*', it is permissible, as here, to use an alternative of your own choice. Attaching the main dream images in order to your alphabet image words in this way allows you easily to span the different brainwave states in which you find yourself when asleep, when waking and when fully awake, thus enabling you to remember that important and very useful part of your paraconscious life.

The benefits of being able to recall dreams

Numerous studies of people who have started to remember their dreams show that, over a period of months, they become calmer, more motivated, more humorous, more imaginative, more creative and far better able to remember things generally. All of this is not surprising, for your paraconscious dream world is a constant playground for your whole set of cognitive skills, exercising the part of your brain, your cerebral cortex, where all of the 12 memory techniques are practised to perfection. Getting in touch with these at the *conscious* level encourages all the connected skills to improve automatically.

An example of dream memorisation showing the key main images

If, as many people do, you become interested in this area of self-exploration and improvement, it is useful to keep a 'dream diary'. Such a diary will give you constant practice in all the skills mentioned and become an increasingly useful tool in your overall self-development. After a little practice you may well find yourself both appreciating and creating literature and art at levels you had not previously explored.

Many famous people have used such a process. Edgar Allan Poe, for example, first remembered and then used the more night-marish of his dreams as the basis for his short horror stories. Similarly, Salvador Dali, the surrealist artist, publicly stated that many of his paintings were reproductions of perfectly remembered images from his dreams.

Now let's return to the waking world and explore the ultimate method for increasing the power of your memory, your focus and your creativity. For the more adventurous, the next section shows you how, using a system that helps you to memorise it, you can develop 10,000 pegs for things you want to remember. That system is the self-enhancing master memory matrix, (or, SEM^3 for short). SEM^3 will enable you to memorise a vast range of information for the purposes of study, business or simply leisure and self-improvement. Part 4, which follows, explains SEM^3 in detail and shows you how to use and apply it to a variety of learning categories.

Tony's self-enhancing **master memory matrix system** is superior to just list learning for a party trick . . . it is **building encyclopaedic knowledge**: it builds knowledge on knowledge.

Dr Sue Whiting, five times Women's World Memory Champion and first-ever female Grand Master of Memory (GMM)

Part 4

The total learning memory technique

Part 4 introduces you to the final great memory enhancement technique developed in the last millennium: the self-enhancing master memory matrix, hereafter referred to simply as SEM³. This technique will allow you to memorise an unlimited number of items with comparative ease. At the same time, you will be also exercising your 'memory muscle', improving your imagination and sharpening all your senses.

The self-enhancing master memory matrix (SEM³)

SEM³ allows you – by expanding on the memory systems covered in Parts 2 and 3 – to use 10,000 distinct and ordered memory pegs to learn an infinite amount of information as quickly as you can visualise it.

Dr Sue Whiting, the foremost proponent of this technique, explains the basic premise of SEM³. Her words are followed by an 'insider's' approach to mastering the technique.

> *'All those who are seriously interested in improving their memories, and that should mean everyone because we all have memories that can be improved, should try using SEM³. On my first introduction to the technique it took me completely by surprise. You certainly do need to apply yourself with determination to get started with learning SEM³. Having said that, I had no idea that memorising information could be such fun! After all, revising for exams was always tedious and, dare I say it, boring. Suddenly, memorising became both possible*

and pleasurable, and expanding my memory developed into a hobby.

Using this memory technique led on to other things, but it was certainly not a case of memorising for the sake of it. There is a basic step-by-step approach to SEM³ that is worth remembering. Work through the following lists as described below and you will find it very satisfying.'

How does it work?

SEM³ uses the ice cube idea explored earlier (see Chapter 8). In this system, however, it is done in such a highly refined and structured way that it enables you effortlessly to retrieve vast amounts of information. You will effectively become a human encyclopaedia, being able to access information in a methodical and almost super-computer-like way by simply thinking of a specific memory image word.

The method is based on the initial 100 memory image words used in the major system learned in Chapter 9. The major system may be considered to be in two dimensions, whereas SEM³ adds another dimension, to become a limitless three-dimensional structure. If you have reached this part of the book, your memory will have become so refined and sophisticated that you will be able to superimpose subtle changes on those initial 100 major system images and retrieve, in a very methodical way, all the information stored on any one of those slightly different pegs.

It is a prerequisite that you know the major system as well as you knew (or should have known!) your multiplication tables at school. Your different images for the basic 100 numbers should be automatic. Having progressed to this part of the book you should never need to work out a memory image word. For example, if I said, 84, you should instantly know that this is 'fair'. You shouldn't need to work out that 8 is f, 4 is R and the first vowel sound is an 'A' spelled 'ai'. If you still have to go through this process (which is akin to a child mentally counting all the way up the 8 times table to get 6 × 8 is 48) it will slow you down and may even be confused with the actual new information you want to learn.

To create the system of 10,000, the major system's initial 100 images are simply used in 100 different ways, incorporating all of your senses of vision, sound, smell, taste, touch and sensation, as well as basic data from the physical kingdoms. If you think of the major system as being in two dimensions, then you can probably visualise how SEM³ is in three. It really is incredibly powerful.

By creating a system using such elements, you are at the same time using all of those aspects of your brain that feed your memory skills. You are creating a giant three-dimensional mental gymnasium. This will allow you to memorise any list you wish and also provide you with ongoing mental workouts that increase every aspect of your 'memory muscle' while playing infinite games.

You construct your SEM³ in the following manner.

000–999	Vision
1000–1999	Sound
2000–2999	Smell
3000–3999	Taste
4000–4999	Touch
5000–5999	Sensation
6000–6999	Animals
7000–7999	Birds
8000–8999	The rainbow
9000–9999	The solar system

For the numbers 0 to 999, you use *vision* – in other words, you focus on *seeing* the images you wish to remember as your key means of remembering them. For 1000 to 1999, you use sound – focusing on *hearing* with each image. For 2000 to 2999, you use your sense of *smell* – focusing on this sense in your memory images. So you continue, for each thousand, using, sequentially, taste, touch, sensation, animals, birds, the colours of the rainbow and the solar system.

For each group of 100 within each 1000, you assign a specific vision, a specific sound, a specific smell, and so on. Thus, referring to the matrix shown on page 185, your specific visions for the separate 100s from 0 to 999 are see, dinosaur, nobility, moonlight, ravine, lightning, church, Concorde, fire and painting.

To help you remember this you will notice that the first letter of each of these words corresponds to the consonant sounds of the major system (see the major system's special code in Chapter 9).

An example of SEM³ in action

For example 101 corresponds to 1 in the list of the initial 101 memory image words for the major system so might simply be a giant dinosaur with its head rising above the horizon next to the sun at the beginning of a new *day*, while 140 would correspond to 40 so your same dinosaur could be leading an incredibly noisy, thundering and exciting dinosaur *race*. Whatever you wish to memorise as your 101st or 140th items would be attached to these SEM³ images using the SMASHIN' SCOPE 12 memory techniques on page 33.

Progressing through the first 1000 in the table that use vision, all items from 700 to 799 would use the major system's initial 101 memory image words again (from 1 to 100), but now connected to the image of *Concorde*. Thus, 706 might be Concorde with its bent nose as a giant *jaw* and 795 could be Concorde with a giant *ball* for its wheels. Again, any item you wish to attach to these images would be attached using the 12 memory techniques.

Similarly, for 3000 to 3999, each separate 100 in the progression would have a taste image attached, in the order spaghetti, tomato, nuts, mango, rhubarb, lemon, cherry, custard, fudge and banana.

When playing the game of creating your images make sure that, in your memory images for each of the different senses concerned, you emphasise the sense. For example 4143 damp (for your sense of touch) is combined with the major system's memory image word ram (for 43). It's crucial that you really feel the wetness of the ram's coat, its horns, its muzzle and even the smell of damp wool.

Thousands		0–99	100–199	200–299	300–399	400–499	500–599	600–699	700–799	800–899	900–999
100–999	Vision	–	Dinosaur	Nobility	Moonlight	Ravine	Lightning	Church	Concorde	Fire	Painting
1000–1999	Sound	Sing	Drum	Neigh	Moan	Roar	Lap	Shh	Gong	Violin	Piano
2000–2999	Smell	Seaweed	Tar	Nutmeg	Mint	Rose	Leather	Cheese	Coffee	Forest	Bread
3000–3999	Taste	Spaghetti	Tomato	Nuts	Mango	Rhubarb	Lemon	Cherry	Custard	Fudge	Banana
4000–4999	Touch	Sand	Damp	Newspaper	Mud	Rock	Lather	Jelly	Grass	Velvet	Bark
5000–5999	Sensation	Swimming	Dancing	Nuzzling	Mingling	Rubbing	Loving	Shaking	Climbing	Flying	Peace
6000–6999	Animals	Zebra	Dog	Newt	Monkey	Rhinoceros	Elephant	Giraffe	Kangaroo	Fox	Bear
7000–7999	Birds	Seagull	Duck	Nightingale	Magpie	Robin	Lark	Chicken	Kingfisher	Flamingo	Peacock
8000–8999	Rainbow	Red	Orange	Yellow	Green	Blue	Indigo	Violet	Black	Grey	White
9000–9999	Solar system	Sun	Mercury	Venus	Earth	Mars	Jupiter	Saturn	Uranus	Neptune	Pluto

The self-enhancing master memory matrix (SEM³)

The benefits of SEM³

By using SEM³, you will be developing a system that enables you to memorise an unlimited number of items on 10,000 memory hooks and also be training each one of your sensory areas. This will have a profound and positive influence on all other aspects of your life, including your health. The inability to remember – and the subsequent frustration and annoyance experienced – can lead to stress and even illness. This creates a downward spiral, worsening memory. By using SEM³, you will be reversing such a trend.

In many ways you will be creating a positive spiral as the more you practise your memory techniques, the more your general memory will improve; the more you add your knowledge lists to your memory matrix, the more you will be increasing the probability of automatic learning and the more you do all this, the more automatically all of your various intelligences and mental skills will be improved.

To get you off to a good start, I have selected the first part of two of the lists that appear with other lists on the dedicated website at **www.pearson-books.com/thebuzanmemorybook**.

These lists, once they are learnt, will form giant foundations on which your brain can continue to build its way to wisdom. Your brain will be provided with enough units of organised data to set your 'memory engine' on course for automatic growth! Of course there are many other 'master lists' to which you can apply your memory processes.

The suggested approach for learning any lists is to organise your SEM³ appropriately, before commencing the exercise of remembering them. Throughout, apply the SMASHIN' SCOPE 12 memory techniques.

From this point on, it is useful to develop further memory matrices for any other lists that would be useful to you and to make a habit of memorising at least one new list per year.

Applying SEM³ to a sample list

Dr Sue Whiting, GMM, five times Women's World Memory Champion, has memorised well over 5000 bits of data using SEM³ and uses the SEM³ locations shown in the table opposite for some of the major areas of her knowledge:

SEM³ sections	Categories
1000–1199	Geniuses
1200–1399	Artists
1400–1599	Composers
1600–1799	Scientists
1800–1999	Writers
2000–2099	Monarchs
4000–4099	Geography
5000–5999	Languages
7000–7499	Shakespeare
8000–8199	The elements
8200–8599	The human body
9000–10,000+!	Your life

SEM³ Illustration 1: Learning about famous writers

To illustrate how this all works in practice, the table below gives you a short list of writers and their dates for you to learn. An extensive list of 100 writers may be found on the Web at **www.pearson-books.com/ thebuzanmemorybook.com**, and here we are going to give you the first 32 (see page 188).

Writers are more than simply clever users of words. They may be more accurately described as investigators of all fields of human knowledge, using words as their major investigative tool.

When you explore the world of literature, you also explore the worlds of psychology, geography, philosophy, history, astronomy, economics, mathematics, politics, biology, physics, exploration, imagination and fantasy. Therefore, as you build up your 'master memory matrix' of the great writers, you will be simultaneously extending a multiplicity of associative grappling hooks into all realms of human knowledge. With every author and literary work you come to know, your ability to link with every other author and every other work will increase. This increase in knowledge will have as its automatic companions an increase in your speed of learning and an increase in your enjoyment of language, literature and life.

1	Geoffrey Chaucer	1340–1400
2	Edmund Spenser	1552–1599
3	Sir Walter Raleigh	1552–1618
4	Francis Bacon	1561–1626
5	William Shakespeare	1564–1616
6	Christopher Marlowe	1564–1593
7	John Donne	1572–1631
8	Ben Jonson	1572–1637
9	John Milton	1608–1674
10	John Bunyan	1628–1688
11	John Dryden	1631–1700
12	Samuel Pepys	1633–1703
13	Daniel Defoe	1660–1731
14	Jonathan Swift	1667–1745
15	Joseph Addison	1672–1719
16	George Berkeley	1685–1753
17	Alexander Pope	1688–1744
18	Samuel Richardson	1689–1761
19	Benjamin Franklin	1706–1790
20	Henry Fielding	1707–1754
21	Samuel Johnson	1709–1784
22	Thomas Gray	1716-1771
23	Oliver Goldsmith	1728-1774
24	Edmund Burke	1729–1797
25	William Cowper	1731–1800
26	James Boswell	1740–1795
27	Fanny Burney	1752–1840
28	George Crabbe	1754–1832
29	William Blake	1757–1827
30	Robert Burns	1759–1796
31	William Cobbett	1762–1835
32	William Wordsworth	1770–1850

Learning the writers' names

From the previous table you can see that writers have been allocated the section 1800–1999 in Dr Sue Whiting's SEM³ locations.

Your next step is to use SEM³ to find what needs to be superimposed on the initial 100 major system images to create memory pegs for the writers' details. Start by going down the column on the far left of the table, setting out the memory image words for the groups of thousands and hundreds on page 185 and stop when you reach the box for 1000–1999. The box to the right of it says 'Sound'. Continue to follow this line across the table until you reach the last two boxes, which are 'Violin' and 'Piano'. Thus, any facts that you want to learn about the writers will need to use the usual major system's initial images for 1 to 100 with the sound of violins superimposed on them for the first 100 writers and the sound of a piano superimposed on them for the second 100 writers. As you have found the slot you need for writers, you don't need to look at this SEM³ table again until you wish to learn a different category of information.

Before you progress further, just think about the huge diversity of violin sounds you could use ranging from your favourite concerto to a violinist tuning up the A string. You don't have to use the same violin sound for every writer.

The next step is to find a mnemonic for each writer's name. You need to attach these mnemonics to their major system's image's with the violin sounds.

Here are four examples with some of my suggestions to get you started. This leaves you a further 28 to try out for yourself.

1 Geoffrey Chaucer
   The image for '1' in the major system is 'day'. You may decide to use the beginning of a beautiful day – daybreak – for this image. An image of a friend called Geoffrey with a saucer for (Chaucer) on top of his head, perhaps. Then you simply link the images together using the SMASHIN' SCOPE 12 memory techniques. Hear violins (and probably birds joining in as well to reinforce the daybreak picture but the violins must still be the dominant sound) as you see the dawn followed by the sun rising. Geoffrey then enters your mental picture, staggering around because he is trying to balance a giant (colourful) saucer on his head. Try to make it feel as though you're actually there with your crazy friend

Geoffrey, experiencing the fantastic daybreak, with the violins and birds.

15 Joseph Addison

As the memory image word for the number 15 in the major system is 'dale', you need to picture a dale and at the same time 'hear' the sound of a violin.

The next stage is to think of a mnemonic for Joseph Addison. How about the biblical Joseph adding in the sun? The amazing thing is that, as long as you remember to 'hear' the sound of violins when you memorise Joseph Addison interacting with the dale you'll find it really easy to access this data later and you'll be able to keep it quite distinct from the dale that has a roaring sound, a neighing sound or a piano. Remember the SMASHIN' SCOPE 12 memory techniques. Try to really *feel* the hot sunshine. Is he using his toes or an abacus for the adding? What is your dale like? Perhaps it's very lush and you can smell the grass very distinctly. Try to make Joseph's clothes colourful, too. The more that you are involved and the more information you include in this mental image the more memorable and fun it will be.

19 Benjamin Franklin

The number 19 corresponds to a *dab* on the Major system. You might use the mnemonic '*bend them in and frank them*' for Benjamin Franklin. So the next step is to have violins playing while dabs are being bent to be fed into a franking machine. One dab alone is rather boring! A pile of dabs going into the franking machine will make a better image **than just one dab** as there will be more action. Just remember that you are memorising the two- not three-digit number. Now you've reached this part of the book you are such an expert memoriser that you are allowed to bend the rules.

32 William Wordsworth

The number 32 is 'man' in the major system so you may decide to use superman for your image because he's very colourful in his blue and red outfit.

You could use an orange to remember the name William because of William of Orange.

The final step is to put all this together. So, have the violins playing as superman flies past on an enormous orange. Emblazoned on his chest is the name 'WORDSWORTH'.

Now you can see how easy it is, try to memorise the remaining writers. When you start doing this you may find it easier to set yourself a target of about five a day. You'll still be able to complete the list in less than a week. It's often a good idea to review your list of writers whenever you're waiting for a train, standing in a queue and so on. Then you will have used this otherwise wasted time in a very efficient way, and improved your ability to recall the list.

Learning the writers' dates

Once you know all 32 writers names, you can than go through the list again, this times linking their names, already attached to their appropriate major system peg words with violins, with their dates. You'll find that doing it this way (instead of learning everything about a particular writer in one go), linking new information to the old, will lodge the previous information you've learned even more firmly in your memory.

The method for remembering dates is simple and has been covered earlier in this book. You will recall that you make a word or string of words from the major system consonants used to represent the numbers of the date. Let's explore three different ways to achieve this for Geoffrey Chaucer, 1340–1400.

Convert to consonants using the major system's special code and make a memorable word or phrase

With this method it's usually best to drop the first '1' so you have:

3 M
4 R
0 S/Z
4 R
0 S/Z
0 S/Z

Perhaps you could use the phrase, 'Makes really saucy reading szzzz szzzz'.

This phrase then needs to be linked to daybreak with violins playing and Geoffrey with the saucer on his head. So, you could 'hear' Geoffrey saying this phrase or it could be written on the saucer.

When this method works – such as using 'Crashing Choral Symphony' for Beethoven's date of birth, 1770 (see Chapter 14) it's absolutely brilliant. Some cases may take you longer than others to work out a suitable phrase for. If you have trouble, the following methods using the major system (either the initial 101 memory image words list or the list for numbers 101 to 1000), although not as imaginative, may prove to be quicker and easier for you.

Using the initial 101 memory image words for the major system

At first you may find it easier to include the '1' of the dates because you'll have four images (each representing a two-digit number) to memorise – that is, two images per date. For example:

13 dam
40 race
14 dairy
00 saw

Now connect these new bits of data to your image for the name using the link system. It's very simple and very effective.

Perhaps while your violins are tuning up and the birds start their dawn chorus Geoffrey enters with a saucer on his head. This time, though, he's actually charging across a dam, taking part in a 'saucer-on-the-head' race (a variant of an egg-and–spoon race!) Cows (for dairy) hold the finishing line ribbon. Unfortunately, the ribbon is so strong that Geoffrey is unable to break it as he runs through, so he *saws* his way through it to become the winner. In this way you have included 'dam', 'race', 'dairy' and 'saw' to give 1340 and 1400. The disadvantage, however, is that you've learned three unnecessary digits. As a result, you may decide to delete the '1' at the beginning of each of the two dates and use the second list for the major system, as we shall see next.

Using the second list for the major system

This is even simpler than the previous methods as you would only then need to memorise *two* images:

340 Mars
400 recess, but use roses to make it easier.

Perhaps Geoffrey could be sitting on a flying saucer, on his way to Mars, where he discovers the reason that it's red is because it's covered with red roses.

Reinforcing and extending your learning

Whichever method you choose, try to do frequent reviews at odd moments during the day by just quickly flashing through everything you've learned. If you can't remember something, you can always check with the book later and make the images stronger using the SMASHIN' SCOPE 12 memory techniques. In addition you'll have been able to review and strengthen all the others.

More details about each of the first 32 writers follow (for details of the remaining 68 writers, visit the website, as before). This is so that, once you have finished attaching the writers' dates to their names, you can add any other information in exactly the same way. If you want to remember their nationalities, say work out a mnemonic and link it in to your scenarios.

Returning to Geoffrey Chaucer, for example, after you have learned the image of him finding red roses on Mars, you subsequently add a bulldog (a mnemonic for British nationality) that suddenly comes bounding up to him.

Have fun!!

1 **Geoffrey Chaucer 1340–1400** *Nationality*: British.
Famous work: The Canterbury Tales.
Educated: London.
Notes: Known as the 'Father of English Literature'.

2 **Edmund Spenser 1552–1599** *Nationality*: British.
Famous works: The Faerie Queene, Colin Clout's Come Home Againe.
Educated: Merchant Taylors' School, Northampton, then Cambridge.
Notes: Often called 'Father of the English Fairytale'.

3   **Sir Walter Raleigh**   1552–1618   *Nationality*: British.
Famous works: *The History of the World*, *The Discoverie of the Large, Rich and Beautiful Empyre of Guiana*.
Educated: Oxford (Law).
Notes: An explorer and adventurer who led expeditions to America and South America. He had an enquiring mind and an uncommon literary ability.

4   **Francis Bacon (Lord Verulam)**   1561–1626   *Nationality*: British.
Famous work: *The Advancement of Learning*.
Educated: Trinity College, Cambridge (Law).
Notes: Had unquenchable curiosity about nature of the world and behaviour of his fellow men.

5   **William Shakespeare**   1564–1616   *Nationality*: British.
Famous works: *Othello, King Lear, Macbeth, Antony and Cleopatra*, and many more.
Educated: Holy Trinity Church, Stratford
Notes: Most prolific period, 1604–1608. It was said of him that 'he is not of an age but for all time'.

6   **Christopher Marlowe**   1564–1593   *Nationality*: British.
Famous work: 'The Passionate Shepherd to His Love'.
Educated: Corpus Christi College, Cambridge.
Notes: Died from stabbing during fight with friends while gambling on backgammon.

7   **John Donne**   1572–1631   *Nationality*: British
Famous works: *Devotions, Elegies and Sonnets*.
Educated: Oxford and Cambridge.
Notes: One of the Metaphysical poets; became Dean of St Paul's in 1621 and wrote 160 sermons.

8   **Ben Jonson**   1572–1637   *Nationality*: British
Famous works: Volpone, Bartholomew Fayre, Timber.
Educated: Westminster School
Notes: Leader of new generation of poets known as 'The Tribe of Ben'.

9 **John Milton   1608–1674**   *Nationality*: British
Famous works: Paradise Lost, 'On His Blindness', *Il Penseroso*
Educated: Christ's College, Cambridge.
Notes: The Civil War diverted his energies to the parliamentary and political struggle. Wrote *Paradise Lost* and 'On His Blindness' after he had become blind.

10 **John Bunyan   1628–1688**   *Nationality*: British
Famous works: The Pilgrim's Progress, Grace Abounding to the Chief of Sinners.
Educated: Village school, Elstow.
Notes: He wrote *The Pilgrim's Progress* while imprisoned for 12 years for unlicensed preaching.

11 **John Dryden   1631–1700**   *Nationality*: British
Famous works: Marriage à la Mode, The Rehearsal.
Educated: Westminster School and Trinity College, Cambridge.
Notes: Poet Laureate in 1668.

12 **Samuel Pepys   1633–1703**   *Nationality*: British
Famous work: Diary.
Educated: St Paul's School and Magdalene College, Cambridge.
Notes: Diary not deciphered until 1825.

13 **Daniel Defoe   1660–1731**   *Nationality*: British
Famous work: Robinson Crusoe.
Educated: Stoke Newington Academy.
Notes: Most prolific after age of 60; dubbed 'founder of English journalism'.

14 **Jonathan Swift   1667–1745**   *Nationality*: British
Famous work: Gulliver's Travels.
Educated: Kilkenny School and Trinity College, Dublin.
Notes: From age 23, suffered from Ménière's disease.

15 **Joseph Addison   1672–1719**   *Nationality*: British
Famous work: Cato.
Educated: Charterhouse School and Magdalen College, Oxford.
Notes: Member of Parliament.

16 **George Berkeley**   1685–1753   *Nationality*: Irish
Famous works: An Essay Towards a New Theory of Vision, Alciphron.
Educated: Trinity College, Dublin.
Notes: First published works were tracts on mathematics, written in Latin.

17 **Alexander Pope**   1688–1744   *Nationality*: British
Famous works: The Rape of the Lock and translations of Homer's *The Iliad* and *Odyssey*.
Educated: Self-educated.
Notes: Suffered from ill-health most of his life.

18 **Samuel Richardson**   1689–1761   *Nationality*: British
Famous works: Pamela, Clarissa.
Educated: Grew up in poverty, education sketchy.
Notes: Obsessed with sex, which led to the popularity of his writings. Regarded as 'one of the founders of the modern novel'.

19 **Benjamin Franklin**   1706–1790   *Nationality*: American
Famous works: Observation on the Relationships of Britain to her Colonies, Rules by which a Great Empire may be Reduced to a Small One.
Educated: Born Boston, education sketchy.
Notes: Scientist and politician; helped draft the American Constitution. Founded the influential social and debating society the Junto Club.

20 **Henry Fielding**   1707–1754   *Nationality*: British
Famous works: Tom Jones, The History of the Adventures of Joseph Andrews and His Friend, Mr Abraham Abrams.
Educated: Eton.
Notes: Very sick much of his life with asthma and dropsy.

21 **Samuel Johnson**   1709–1784   *Nationality*: British
Famous works: Dictionary, The Vanity of Human Wishes.
Educated: Pembroke College, Oxford.
Notes: Famous lexicographer, critic, brilliant conversationalist and wit.

22 Thomas Gray 1716–1771 *Nationality*: British
Famous work: 'Elegy Written in a Country Churchyard'.
Educated: Eton and Peterhouse College, Cambridge.
Notes: Letters are among finest in the English language – incredible descriptive powers and wit.

23 Oliver Goldsmith 1728–1774 *Nationality*: Irish
Famous works: The Vicar of Wakefield, She Stoops to Conquer, The Citizen of the World.
Educated: Trinity College, Dublin.
Notes: In his own words, he was mostly addicted to gambling and was an experienced liar.

24 Edmund Burke 1729–1797 *Nationality*: Irish
Famous work: Reflections on the Revolution in France.
Educated: Quakers School, Balitore, and Trinity College, Dublin.
Notes: Whig politician and political theorist. Founded *The Annual Register.*

25 William Cowper 1731–1800 *Nationality*: British
Famous works: Table Talk, The Task.
Educated: Westminster School, The Inner Temple (Law).
Notes: Trained as a lawyer and was converted to evangelical Christianity.

26 James Boswell 1740–1795 *Nationality*: Scottish
Famous work: The Life of Dr Johnson.
Educated: Edinburgh University (Law).
Notes: Felt thwarted because he did not attain the political career he wanted.

27 Fanny Burney 1752–1840 *Nationality*: British
Famous works: Evelina, Cecilia, Camilla.
Educated: Self-educated.
Notes: Her diary is one of the best first-hand portraits of late eighteenth-century characters and life.

28 George Crabbe 1754–1832 *Nationality*: British
Famous work: The Village.
Educated: Apprentice to a doctor.
Notes: Narrative poet of grim humour.

29 **William Blake   1757–1827**   *Nationality*: British
Famous works: Songs of Innocence and Experience, The Marriage of Heaven and Hell, Jerusalem.
Educated: Royal Academy at Somerset House.
Notes: Volumes of meaning expressed in apparently simple, musical lines of his poetry.

30 **Robert Burns   1759–1796**   *Nationality*: Scottish
Famous works: 'Tam-o'Shanter', 'Auld Lang Syne', 'To a Mouse'.
Educated: By his father and mother.
Notes: Scotland's national poet, wrote most remarkable cantata, 'The Jolly Beggar'.

31 **William Cobbett ('Peter Porcupine')   1762–1835**
Nationality: British
Famous works: Rural Rides, Cobbett's Political Register, Porcupine's Gazette.
Educated: Self-educated in army.
Notes: His published output was enormous, from farming to politics.

32 **William Wordsworth   1770–1850**   *Nationality*: British
Famous works: 'I wandered lonely as a cloud' (commonly known as 'Daffodils'), *Sonnets*, 'Ode: Intimations of Immortality', *The Prelude*.
Educated: Hawkshead Grammar School and St John's College, Cambridge.
Notes: Born in the English Lake District; a leading Romantic poet.
See **www.pearson-books.com/thebuzanmemorybook**.

SEM³ Illustration 2: learning about the great composers

You will find below a list of some of the great classical composers, which you can use to test your memory storage capacity using SEM³. On its own, the list will provide your brain with enough units of organised data to set your 'memory engine' on course for natural growth.

I have chosen to list composers because this engages many areas of knowledge, and I could just as easily have created a list of geniuses, artists, scientists, rulers of the world, countries and capital cities, the elements or the solar system. (For more memory lists, go online to **www.pearson-books.com/thebuzanmemory book**. If you want to take a look.)

Once you have organised and memorised, using SEM[3], the following list of composers and the key bits of information about them, you will have created a foundation for your musical knowledge that will allow your brain automatically to build multiple associations around each composer and each composer's music, rapidly integrating those into a growing fabric of delightful and spirit-enhancing knowledge.

When you hear, for example, that Smetana was originally known for his astounding energy and enthusiasm, his two children died at an early age and he lost his life to a most debilitating disease, which caused the physical disintegration of his brain, yet he still composed and recorded in intricate detail the nature of his decline and the nature of its effect on his memory, you will listen to his music with greater understanding and compassion. Similarly you will know more about the historical times in which he lived.

Learning the composers' details

If you look again at Dr Sue Whiting's SEM[3] locations on page 187, you'll see that composers have been allocated the section 1400–1599.

Again you need to use SEM[3] to find what you need to superimpose on the major system's memory image words to create memory pegs for the great composers. Start by looking down the column on the far left of the table on page 185 once more and stop when you reach the box for 1000–1999. The box to the right of it says 'Sound'. Continue to follow this line across the table until you reach the boxes, 'Roar' and 'Lap' Thus, any facts that you want to learn about the composers will need to use the usual major system's initial images for 1 to 100 with a roaring sound superimposed on them for the first 100 writers and a lapping sound superimposed on them for the second 100.

Sound is a major memory device. It is also one of the areas of mental skill that is essential for the development of the master memory skill of 'synaesthesia' – the blending of the senses for the enhancement of each and the correlated increase in mental skills that results, especially creativity and memory. You'll be surprised how, just by thinking of a different sound and attaching it to any major system hook, you will be able to access totally different pieces of information.

Let's see how this works in practise by looking at how the system is used for the first entry in the list.

1 Philippe de Vitry 1291–1361

Think of a mnemonic for Philippe de Vitry to attach to *day* using a *roar.*

You may think of the London *PHIL*harmonic orchestra which is performing in the branches of a *V*-shaped tree. You could then link this in to a roaring daybreak scene.

Completing your learning of the list

Below is a list of 30 composers to get you started on the way to your knowledge of the great composers.

Ensure that you have a roaring sound before you attach your mnemonic for each composer's name on to its major system hook.

Once you've learned all 30 names, go through the list again, this time adding their dates, using whichever method you prefer. Only add their nationalities once their dates are firmly in your memory, then continue, repeatedly going through the list and adding more information to your hooks every time.

1 **Philippe de Vitry**   1291–1361   *Nationality*: French.
Famous work: *Impudenter circumivi/Virtutibus.*
Style: Secular and of the Ars Nova.
Era: Middle Ages

2 **Guillaume de Machaut**   1300–1377   *Nationality*: French.
Famous work: *Messe de Notre Dame.*
Style: Sacred and secular
Notes: Well-respected statesman, cleric and poet
Era: Middle Ages.

3 Francesco Landini   1325–1397   *Nationality*: Italian
Famous work: *'Ecco la primavera'*.
Style: Secular.
Notes: Blind from childhood.
Era: Middle Ages.

4 John Dunstable   1390–1453   *Nationality*: English
Famous work: 'O Rosa Bella'.
Style: Sacred and secular.
Notes: Well-known for 'singability' of his music
Era: Middle Ages

5 Gilles de Bins Binchois   1400–1460   *Nationality*: Franco-Flemish
Famous work: 'Filles à marier'.
Style: Sacred and secular.
Era: Renaissance.

6 Guillaume Dufay   1400–1474   *Nationality*: Franco-Flemish
Famous work: 'Se la face ay pale'.
Style: Sacred and secular
Era: Renaissance.

7 Johannes Ockeghem   1410–1497   *Nationality*: Franco-Flemish
Famous work: *Missa cuiusvi toni*.
Style: Sacred and secular.
Era: Renaissance.

8 Josquin Desprez   1440–1521   *Nationality*: Franco-Flemish
Famous work: 'Ave Maria'.
Style: Sacred and secular.
Era: Renaissance.

9 Heinrich Isaac   1450–1517   *Nationality*: Flemish
Famous work: *Choralis constantinus*.
Style: Sacred and secular vocal music.
Era: Renaissance.

10 Andrea Gabrieli   1510–1586   *Nationality*: Italian
Famous work: *Magnificat for three choirs and orchestra*.
Style: Sacred and madrigals.
Notes: Introduced the technique 'Cori spezzati' (spaced choirs).
Era: Renaissance.

11 **Giovanni Pierluigi da Palestrina** 1525–1594 *Nationality*: Italian
Famous work: *'Missa Papae Marcelli'*.
Style: Sacred and secular vocal music.
Era: Renaissance.

12 **Orlande de Lassus** 1532–1594 *Nationality*: Franco-Flemish
Famous work: 'Alma redemptoris mater'.
Style: Sacred and secular vocal music.
Era: Renaissance.

13 **William Byrd** 1543–1623 *Nationality*: English
Famous work: 'Sing Joyfully'/'Ave Verum Corpus'.
Style: Sacred and secular choral music, vocal chamber music,
instrumental and keyboard music.
Notes: Described as 'Father of British music'.
Era: Renaissance.

14 **Giulio Caccini** 1545–1618 *Nationality*: Italian
Famous work: 'Toccate d'Intavolature di Cimbale e Organo'.
Style: Le Nuove Musiche
Era: Baroque.

15 **Tomás Luis de Victoria** 1548–1611 *Nationality*: Spanish
Famous work: *Missa Laetatus Sum*.
Style: Songs in new styles.
Era: Renaissance.

16 **Luca Marenzio** 1553–1599 *Nationality*: Italian
Famous work: 'Dolorosi martir'.
Style: Secular vocal music and sacred vocal music.
Era: Renaissance.

17 **Giovanni Gabrieli** 1555–1612 *Nationality*: Italian
Famous work: 'Canzon XIII'.
Style: Sacred vocal music, instrumental music and secular
vocal music.
Era: Renaissance.

18 **Thomas Morley** 1557–1602 *Nationality*: English
Famous work: 'Now Is the Month of Maying'.
Style: Secular and sacred vocal music, instrumental music.
Notes: Specialised in Ballett Madrigals (light form of madrigal).
Era: Renaissance.

19 Carlo Gesualdo   1560–1613   *Nationality*: Italian
Famous work: 'Deh, coprite il bel seno'.
Style: Secular and sacred vocal music.
Era: Renaissance.

20 John Bull   1562–1628   *Nationality*: English
Famous work: 'Fantasia'.
Style: Keyboard composer.
Era: Renaissance.

21 John Dowland   1563–1626   *Nationality*: English
Famous work: 'In darkness let me dwell'.
Style: Secular vocal, instrumental music.
Era: Renaissance.

22 Claudio Monteverdi   1567–1643   *Nationality*: Italian
Famous works: *Madrigals of Love and War, Il ritorno d'Ulisse in patria (The return of Ulysses to his country)*.
Style: Secular vocal, sacred vocal, madrigals, operas.
Era: Renaissance/Baroque.

23 Thomas Weelkes   1575–1623   *Nationality*: English
Famous work: 'As Vesta was from Latmos Hill descending'.
Style: Madrigals, sacred vocal and instrumental.
Era: Renaissance.

24 Orlando Gibbons   1583–1625   *Nationality*: English
Famous works: 'This is the Record of John', 'The Silver Swan'.
Style: Vocal, sacred choral, keyboard and instrumental music.
Era: Renaissance.

25 Girolamo Frescobaldi   1583–1643   *Nationality*: Italian
Famous work: 'Capriccio sopra la battaglia'.
Style: Vocal and keyboard music.
Notes: Known as 'A giant among organists'.
Era: Baroque.

26 Heinrich Schütz   1585–1672   *Nationality*: German
Famous works: 'St Matthew's Passion', *Christmas Oratorio*.
Style: Secular and sacred vocal music.
Era: Baroque.

27 Francesco Cavalli 1602–1676 *Nationality*: Italian
Famous work: *Ercole Amante (Hercules the Lover)*.
Style: Secular vocal.
Era: Baroque.

28 Giacomo Carissimi 1605–1674 *Nationality*: Italian
Famous work: *The Representation of the Body and Soul.*
Style: Sacred musical dramas.
Era: Baroque.

29 Jean-Baptiste Lully 1632–1687 *Nationality*: Italian
Famous work: 'L'amour médecin'.
Style: Sacred choral, comedy ballet, operas, ballets and dance music.
Era: Baroque

30 Dietrich Buxtehude 1637–1707 *Nationality*: Danish
Famous work: Oratorios, cantatas, organ music.
Style: Invented 'musica recitativa'.
Notes: Began idea of evening music, public concerts in churches and known as great influence on Bach.
Era: Baroque.

By using SEM[3] in this way, you are exploring, with the great historical and current musical brains, the human race's search, through the medium of sound, for an increasing understanding of its own nature. As Dr Sue Whiting sums up:

> 'Having memorised many of the composers, I now understand and can relate better to the period in which they composed. My mind is somehow more focused and I appreciate their music even more. Because I now have a "hook" for each of them in my brain, I can easily add further information.
>
> Artists had never been part of my previous studies, but settling down and learning about them [refer to the list on the website] paid real dividends. For a start, it was enjoyable to learn something completely new to me. When I visited the National Gallery you can imagine my delight when in room after room I discovered paintings I had memorised. I could tell my children all sorts of details about the artists and particular styles – a very satisfying experience, and not just because the children looked on their mother with a new respect.

How I wish that I had discovered these memory techniques earlier in life, before I had to take all my exams! You, the reader, have precisely that opportunity. This book will teach you how to learn in the most enjoyable way – but be warned, it can become quite addictive!'

Conclusion

Now that you have read and worked through *The Memory Book*, practising the techniques and trying the exercises, your memory will, already, be vastly improved. You'll also start developing, because of the skills used in memorisation, the left and right hemispheres of your brain, giving it a total workout. Keep flexing and testing your memory muscles and you'll be amazed at the results – what you're capable of remembering and just how creative and fast-thinking you become.

Whether you wish to master some or all of the basic mnemonic techniques in Part 2, nail the major system in Part 3 or be brave and tackle SEM[3] in Part 4, you have started a journey to maximise your memory capability and your time potential, leading to success in whatever you choose to apply yourself to – be it study, business or leisure.

After mastering all the memory techniques in *The Memory Book*, you may wish to test your memory capabilities against other 'mnemonists' (those who can remember and recall unusually large amounts of data). You can do this by getting involved in the world of the mind sport of memory, for which there are organised events/championships associated with memory training.

In Appendix 1 you can find out how the World Memory Championships came into being, read about some amazing memory feats and read how you too can be part of this worldwide revolution that is enabling everyone to achieve their greatest potential.

Enjoy your infinite and memorable future!

Appendix 1: The mind sport of memory

How the World Memory Championships began

I have been interested in mind sports, especially chess, from a very young age, both playing in and hoping to organise competitions. It seemed strange to me that there should be competitions for chess, go, bridge, mathematics, crosswords and all manner of puzzle and number and word games, yet for, arguably, the brain's greatest skill area – memory – nothing!

With the publications of *Use Your Head* and *Use Your Memory*, my global travels increased, and I became more and more aware of how everyone was interested in the art and science of memory. *Use Your Memory* became a talking point and provocation, and as the years passed, the pressure for memory championships increased. It was, in a very real sense, *Use Your Memory* that inspired the now global 'memory as a mind sport', and both National and World Memory Championships.

In 1990, I had the great good fortune to meet Grand Master Raymond Keene, the first chess player in British chess history to reach the Grand Master level, and the world's number one simultaneous chess player, chess memorist and chess author (150 books to date and rising) Together, we ran the first World Memory

Championship at the Athenaeum Club, London, in 1991. By 1994, psychologists at the University of London had set 'ceilings' above which they thought no memoriser would ever go, including the challenge of memorising a 30-digit long number, read out only once at a rate of 1 digit every 2 seconds.

By 1995, that ceiling had already been shattered! The human brain was already demonstrating that, in the field of memory, its capacities are far far greater than had been hitherto realised. By 1996, Prince Philipp of Liechtenstein had given the Royal Seal of Approval to the Grand Master of Memory title, echoing Tsar Nicholas of Russia's similar royal bestowing of the Grand Master title to chess.

Already by this time, school and junior championships were being established and the mind sport of memory was flowering on an international basis. This growth has continued. By 2008 memory was truly a global sport, with the seventeenth World Memory Championship being held in and sponsored by the Kingdom of Bahrain and the international intellectual capital company Intelnacom.

The mind sport of memory is both a self-enhancing and healthy hobby, as well as being an amateur sport. At the fun end of memory, informal competitions take place in brain clubs and in other mind sport groups and can take many different forms. At a more competitive level, there are specific disciplines that I created in 1991 when I founded the sport that reflect things we all commonly have to remember. A common competition framework has been laid down for these to enable international competitions to take place. It is currently based on ten memory disciplines as follows.

1   Spoken numbers
    Aim to commit to memory and recall as many spoken numbers as possible.

2   One hour cards
    Aim to commit to memory and recall within a time limit as many separate packs (decks) of 52 playing cards as possible.

3   Historic/future dates
    Aim to commit to memory and recall as many given fictional numerical historic/future dates as possible and link them to the right historic event.

4 **Binary numbers**

Aim to commit to memory as many given binary digits (101101) as possible and recall them perfectly.

5 **Random words**

Aim to commit to memory and recall as many given random words as possible.

6 **Abstract images**

Aim to commit to memory and recall a given sequence of abstract images in as many rows as possible.

7 **Names and faces**

Aim to commit to memory and recall as many given names as possible and link them to the correct faces.

8 **Hour number**

Aim to commit to memory as many given random digits (1, 3, 5, 8, 2, 5) as possible and recall them perfectly in an hour.

9 **Speed number**

Aim to commit to memory as many given random digits (1, 3, 5, 8, 2, 5) as possible and recall them perfectly.

10 **Speed cards**

Aim to commit to memory and recall a single pack (deck) of 52 playing cards in the shortest possible time.

Competition organisers can select one or more of these disciplines for an individual competition. Within each discipline, an organiser can also select the duration of memorisation. At a world championship level, some disciplines, such as cards and number, can have a one-hour memorisation period and a two-hour recall time. At a lower level, memorisation times can be reduced to five minutes, with a ten- or fifteen-minute recall time to suit the level of the competitors taking part.

These types of discipline require experienced arbiters – and time – for marking. Although it is not essential when organising fun memory events and competitions, it is recommended that organisers join the International Guild of Mind Sports Arbiters and take at least the Level One training, to gain invaluable experience that they can use when running their own club or event.

Buzan Brain Clubs

The mind sport of memory is for every age group and every level of experience. It should not be seen in isolation, however, as it is just one of a group of mind sports that can dramatically impact on any individual's mental capacity and skill throughout life.

Brain Clubs, set up by the Buzan organisation, have flourished for many years and bring together Mind Mapping, creativity, IQ, speed reading and memory. Practising each of these disciplines positively impacts on the others. Using Mind Maps, for example, helps with creativity as it presents ideas in a brain-friendly way that inspires new ideas. Also, working on memory techniques makes the brain more capable in every other area, in the same way that working out in a gym builds muscles.

Brain Clubs, whether set up in a school or college, or within an organisation or company, create a supportive environment where all members share the same objective – to give their personal 'necktop computer' the best operating system possible. Buzan Centres worldwide can provide qualified trainers in all of these areas (see **www.buzanworld.com**).

Local competitions in Brain Clubs add excitement and give focus. They also help to create achievement benchmarks that inspire people to perform at their best. Most importantly, they are fun. Out of Brain Clubs come individuals who want to take one or more of the mind sports to a higher level and compete at a regional, national or even international level. There have been competitors at the World Memory Championship who are still at school, so the sport is wide open to everyone.

There is also an increasing number of online fun memory competitions that, equally, are open to everyone. Details of these competitions and the World Memory Championships are carried on the news page of the World Memory Sports Council's website, **www.worldmemorysportscouncil.com**.

The World Memory Sports Council can be contacted by e-mail at: **info@worldmemorysportscouncil.com** or by post at:

General Secretary
World Memory Sports Council
14, Croydon Road
Waddon
Croydon
Surrey CR0 4PA
Telephone: +44 (0)20 8688 2598
Fax: + 44 (0)870 116 3530

As *The Memory Book* goes to print, the World Memory Sports Council, the official ruling body of the memory sports, has a growing number of countries as members. These include, among its major members, Austria, China, France, Germany, Latvia, Mexico, Singapore, India, Australia, United Kingdom and United States of America. National championships are now regularly held. In addition to many national championships, the first Latin American memory championship will be held in Mexico in March 2010. This championship will be organised with the patronage of Tec de Monterrey, one of the world's largest and most highly rated universities, with 39,000 students located in 33 different campuses throughout Latin America.

In addition to the national and world memory championships, there have also been exciting developments in the field of online memory competitions. The 2006 China Memory Championship was co-organised by the Central Youth League, supported by the government of Pudong New Area, the Science Committee of Pudong New Area and Zhangjiang Group Company, the National Youth Working Committee, Adolescent Social Service Centre and Shanghai Taotu Information Technology. In the contest, electronic competition software was used for the first time and proved to be successful. The opening ceremony was held at the Great Hall of the People, Beijing and the competition itself was held in Zhangjiang, Shanghai. As the new *Memory Book* goes to press, China has made a spectacular bid for the 2010 World Memory Championships, an event which, in conjunction with the Festival of the Mind, the hosts are saying will be an Olympics of the Brain, designed to charm and impress the world as does the physical Olympics.

Memory championships for schools

Since it was founded in 1991, the World Memory Championships has created a 'gold standard' for memory based on ten different memory disciplines. A simplified version of these has now been created specially for schools' memory competitions, backed up by a training programme to help teachers teach memory techniques. Run by eight times World Memory Champion, Dominic O'Brien and the Chief Arbiter of the World Memory Championships Phil Chambers, the UK Schools Memory Competition has been created to help pupils discover the mind sport of memory and develop their mental skills to help with their studies (for more information, log on to **www.schoolsmemorychampionships.com**).

To find out more about the mind sport of memory, I recommend *The Mind Sport of Memory Yearbook* (available from the World Memory Sports Councils Website, see page 210) which contains histories, articles by the leading figures from the world of memory sports, including those by national and world champions, reports from national committees, hints and tips for Improving your memory from the best grand masters and world champions, guides as to how to run competitions,and results from all the major competitions held around the world. Its robust Appendix also includes the complete official 2007 World Memory Rankings.

Appendix 2: The Festival of the Mind

The Festival of the Mind is a showcase event for the five learning 'mind sports' of Memory, Speed Reading, IQ, Creativity and Mind Mapping.

The first Festival was held in the Royal Albert Hall in 1995 and was organised by Tony Buzan and Raymond Keene OBE. Since then, the Festival has been held in the UK, alongside the World Memory Championships in Oxford, and in other countries around the world including Malaysia, China and Bahrain. The interest from the public in all the five learning mind sports is growing worldwide so, not surprisingly, the Festival is a big attraction. In fact, an event devoted solely to Mind Maps with Tony Buzan filled the Albert Hall again in 2006.

Each of the mind sports has its own Council to promote, administer and recognise achievement in its field.

The World Memory Sports Council

The World Memory Sports Council is the independent governing body of the Mind Sport of Memory and regulates competitions worldwide. Tony Buzan is the President of the Council. You can visit the website at **www.worldmemorysportscouncil.com**

The World Memory Championships

This is the pre-eminent national and international memory competition where records are continually smashed. For instance, in the 2007 UK Memory Championships Ben Pridmore memorised a single shuffled deck of playing cards in 26.28 seconds, beating the previous World Record of 31.16 seconds set by Andi Bell (for years, memorising a pack of cards in under 30 seconds has been seen as the memory equivalent of beating the four-minute mile in athletics). Full details of the World Memory Championships can be found on the website **www.worldmemorychampionships.com** with its interactive Mind Map designed by Mind Map World Champion Phil Chambers using Buzan's iMindMap.

Memory Championships for Schools

Since it was founded in 1991, the World Memory Championships has created a 'gold standard' for memory based on ten different memory disciplines. A simplified version of these has now been created specifically for schools memory competitions, backed up with a training programme to help teachers to train memory techniques.

In a nationwide educational partnership, consisting of the UK Memory Sports Council, Inspire Education, and national government initiative Aimhigher, students are taught powerful memory techniques which, when put into practice, can provide the intellectual platform for recalling almost anything, instantly. They are passing on these techniques to teachers and pupils at secondary schools throughout the UK – by means of the UK Schools Memory Championships.

Organised by Inspire Education and spearheaded by eight times World Memory Champion Dominic O'Brien and the Chief Arbiter of the World Memory Championships, Phil Chambers, the UK Schools Memory Competition has been created to help pupils discover the mind sport of memory and to develop their mental skills to help their studies. We are in the process of creating a model here in the UK which can be repeated around the world with the goal of eventually establishing the 'World Schools Memory Championships' soon after 2010. For more information, log onto **www.schoolsmemory championships.com**.

Welcome to Tony Buzan's world. Tony Buzan is the inventor of Mind Maps – the most powerful 'thinking tool' of our times. Discover more about Tony himself, and the transformative powers of MIND MAPPING, MEMORY and SPEED READING at **www.buzanworld.com**.

The World Speed Reading Council was established to promote, train and recognise achievements in the field of Speed Reading worldwide. Apart from developing the ability to gain an understanding of large quantities of text in a short time, Speed Reading is one of the five learning 'mind sports' which can be practised competitively. Their website is **www.worldspeedreadingcouncil.com**.

Mind Mapping is a 'Thought Organisation Technique' invented by the international author and expert on the brain, Tony Buzan, in 1971. The World Mind Mapping Council administers and promotes the sport and also awards the prestigious title of Mind Mapping World Champion. The current reigning World

Champion is Phil Chambers. Visit the site at **www.worldmind mappingcouncil.com**.

The Worldwide Brain Club, set up by the Buzan Organisation, encourages the formation of Brain Clubs worldwide. These have flourished for many years and bring together Mind Mapping, Creativity, IQ, Speed Reading and Memory. Practising each of these disciplines positively impacts on the others. Using Mind Maps, for example, helps with creativity as it presents ideas in a brain-friendly way that inspires new ideas. Working on memory techniques makes the brain more capable in every other area in the same way as working out in a gym builds muscles.

Brain Clubs, whether set up in a school or college, or within an organisation or company, create a supportive environment where all the members share the same objective: to give their personal 'neck top computer' the best operating system possible. Buzan Centres worldwide provide qualified trainers in all of these areas. See **www.buzanworld.com** and **www.worldbrainclub.com**.

The Brain Trust is a registered charity which was founded in 1990 by Tony Buzan with one objective: to maximise the ability of each and every individual to unlock and deploy the vast capacity of his or her brain. Its charter includes promoting research into study of thought processes, the investigation of the mechanics of thinking, manifested in learning, understanding, communication, problem-solving, creativity and decision making. In 2008 Professor (Baroness) Susan Greenfield won its 'Brain of the Century' award. Visit **www.braintrust.org.uk**.

The International Academy of Mental World Records at **www.mentalworldrecords.com** exists to recognise the achievements of Mental Athletes around the world. In addition to arbiting world record attempts and awarding certificates of achievement, the Academy is also linked to the

International Festival of the Mind, which, as we have seen, show-cases mental achievements in the five learning mind sports of Memory, Speed Reading, Creativity, Mind Mapping and IQ.

Creativity is defined by Torrance, the doyen of creativity testing, as follows:

'Creativity is a process of becoming sensitive to problems, deficiencies, gaps in knowledge, missing elements, disharmonies and so on; identifying the difficulty; searching for solutions; making guesses or formulating hypotheses about the deficiencies; testing and re-testing these hypotheses and possibly modifying and retesting them; and finally communicating the results.'

All of these five skills positively impact on each other and together they can help any individual to be more effective in whatever they choose to do. All five learning mind sports are featured in the Festival of the Mind. Visit **www.worldcreativitycouncil.com**

Intelligence Quotient (IQ) is one of the five learning 'mind sports' which include Mind Mapping, Creativity, Speed Reading and Memory.

The World IQ Council can be contacted at **www.worldiqcouncil.com** and you can test your IQ on this site as well.

Bibliography

Aiken, E.G., Thomas, G.S., and Shennum, W.A. 'Memory for a lecture: Effects of notes, lecture rate, and information density.' *Journal of Educational Psychology* **67** (3), 439–44, 1975.

Anderson, J.R. *Cognitive Psychology and Its Implications*. Second edition. New York: W.H. Freeman & Co., 1985.

Anderson, J.R. 'Retrieval of propositional information from long-term memory.' *Cognitive Psychology* **6**, 451–74, 1974.

Anokhin, P.K. 'The Forming of Natural and Artificial intelligence.' *Impact of Science on Society*, Vol. XXIII **3**, 1973.

Ashcraft, M.H. *Human memory and cognition.* Glenview, Illinois: Scott, Foresman & Co., 1989.

Atkinson, Richard C., and Shiffrin, Richard M. 'The Control of Short-term Memory.' *Scientific American*, August 1971.

Baddeley, Alan D. *The Psychology of Memory.* New York: Harper & Row, 1976.

Bever, T., and Chiarello, R. 'Cerebral dominance in musicians and non-musicians.' *Science* **185**, 137–9, 1974.

Bloch, Michael. 'Improving Mental Performance' biographical notes. Los Angeles: Tel/Syn, 1990.

Borges, Jorge Luis. *Fictions* (especially 'Funes, the Memorious'). London: J. Calder, 1985.

Bourne, L.E., Jr., Dominowski, R.L., Loftus, E.F., and Healy, A.F. *Cognitive Processes.* Englewood Cliffs, NJ: Prentice-Hall Inc., 1986.

Bower, G.H., and Hilgard, E.R. *Theories of Learning.* Englewood Cliffs, NJ: Prentice-Hall Inc., 1981.

Bower, G.H., Clark, M.C., Lesgold, A.M., and Winzenz, D. 'Hierarchical retrieval schemes in recall of categorized word lists.' *Journal of Verbal Learning and Verbal Behavior* **8**, 323–43, 1969.

Breznitz, Z. 'Reducing the gap in reading performance between Israeli lower- and middle-class first-grade pupils.' *Journal of Psychology* **121** (5), 491–501, 1988.

Brown, Mark. *Memory Matters*. Newton Abbot: David & Charles, 1977.

Brown, R., and McNeil, D. 'The 'Tip-of-the-Tongue' Phenomenon.' *Journal of Verbal Learning and Verbal Behavior* 5, 325–37.

Bugelski, B.R., Kidd, E., and Segmen, J. 'Image as a mediator in one-trial paired-associate learning.' *Journal of Experimental Psychology* 76, 69–73, 1968.

Buzan, Tony. The Mind Set: *Use Your Head, The Memory Book, The Mind Map Book* and *The Speed Reading Book*. All London: BBC Worldwide, 2010.

Buzan, Tony. *WHSmith GCSE Revision Guides* (60)

Buzan, Tony. *Head First, The Power of Creative Intelligence, The Power of Spiritual Intelligence, The Power of Social Intelligence, The Power of Verbal Intelligence, Head Strong, How to Mind Map*. All London: Harper Collins, 2002.

Carew, T.J., Hawkins, R.D., and Kandel, E.R. 'Differential classical conditioning of a defensive withdrawal reflex in Aplysia Californica.' *Science* 219, 397–400, 1983.

Catron, R.M., and Wingenbach, N. 'Developing the potential of the gifted reader.' *Theory into Practice*, 25 (2), 134–140, 1986.

Cooper, L.A., and Shepard, R.N. 'Chronometric studies of the rotation of mental images.' In Chase, W.G. (ed.) *Visual Information Processing*. New York: Academic Press, 1973.

Daehler, M.W., and Bukatko, D. *Cognitive Development*. New York: Alfred A. Knopf, 1985.

De Bono, Edward. *The Use of Lateral Thinking*. London: Jonathan Cape, 1967.

De Bono, Edward. *Mind Pack*. London: Dorling Kindersley, 1995.

De Bono, Edward. *How to Have Creative Ideas*. London: Vermilion, 2007.

De Bono, Edward. *Six Frames for Thinking About Information*. London: Vermilion, 2008.

Domjan, M. and Burkhard, B. *The Principles of Learning and Behavior*. Monterey, Cal.: Brooks/Cole Publishing Co., 1982.

Dryden, Gordon and Vos, Jeanette (eds). *The Learning Revolution*. Sacramento, Cal.: Jalmar Press, 1993.

Edwards, B. *Drawing on the Right Side of the Brain*. Los Angeles: J.P. Tarcher, 1979.

Eich, J., Weingartner, H., Stillman, R.C., and Gillin, J.C. 'State-dependent accessibility of retrieval cues in the retention of a categorized list.' *Journal of Verbal Learning and Verbal Behaviour* **14**, 408–17, 1975.

Erickson, T.C. 'Spread of epileptic discharge.' *Archives of Neurology and Psychiatry* **43**, 429–452, 1940.

Fantino, E., and Logan, C.A. *The Experimental Analysis of Behavior: A Biological Perspective.* San Francisco: WH. Freeman & Co., 1979.

Frase, L.T., and Schwartz, B.J. 'Effect of question production and answering on prose recall.' *Journal of Educational Psychology* **67** (5), 628–35, 1975.

Freidman, A., and Polson, M. 'Hemispheres as independent resource systems: Limited-capacity processing and cerebral specialisation.' *Journal of Experimental Psychology: Human Perception and Performance* **7**, 1031–58, 1981.

Gawain, S. *Creative Visualization.* Toronto: Bantam Books, 1978.

Gazzaniga, M. 'Right hemisphere language following brain bisection: A 20-year perspective.' *American Psychologist* **38** (5), 525–37, 1983.

Gazzaniga, M. *Mind Matters.* Boston: Houghton Mifflin Co., 1988.

Gazzaniga, M. *The Social Brain.* New York: Basic Books Inc., 1985.

Gazzaniga, M. and DeDoux, J.E. *The Integrated Mind.* New York: Plenum Press, 1978.

Gelb, Michael J. *How to Think Like Leonardo da Vinci.* New York: Delacorte Press, 1998.

Gelb, Michael J., and Buzan, Tony. *Lessons from the Art of Juggling.* New York: Harmony Books, 1994.

Glass, A.L., and Holyoak, K.J. *Cognition.* New York: Random House,1986.

Godden, D.R., and Baddeley, A.D. 'Context-dependent memory in two natural environments: On land and under water.' *British Journal of Psychology* **66**, 325–31, 1975.

Good, T.L., and Brophy, J.E. *Educational Psychology.* New York: Holt, Rinehart and Winston, 1980.

Greene, R.L. 'A common basis for recency effects in immediate and delayed recall.' *Journal of Experimental Psychology: Learning, Memory and Cognition* **12** (3), 413–18, 1986.

Greenfield, Susan. *Brainpower: Working Out the Human.* Element Books, 2000.

Greenfield, Susan. *Human Brain: A Guided Tour.* London: Phoenix, 2000.

Greenfield, Susan. *The Private Life of the Brain.* London: Penguin, 2002.

Greenfield, Susan. *Inside the Body.* London: Cassell, 2006.

Greenfield, Susan. *ID: The Quest for Identity in the 21st Century.* London: Sceptre, 2008.

Grof, S. *Beyond the Brain: Birth, Death, and Transcendence in Psycho-therapy.* New York: State University of New York Press, 1985.

Haber, Ralph N. 'How We Remember What We See.' *Scientific American*, 105, May 1970.

Halpern, D.F. *Thought and Knowledge: An Introduction to Critical Thinking.* Hillsdale, NJ: Erlbaum, 1984.

Hampton-Turner, C. *Maps of the Mind.* New York: Collier Books, 1981.

Harrison, James. *Max your Brain.* London: Dorling Kindersley, 2010.

Hearst, E. *The First Century of Experimental Psychology.* Hillsdale, NJ: Lawrence Erlbaum Associates, 1979.

Hellige, J. 'Interhemispheric interaction: Models, paradigms and recent findings. In D. Ottoson (ed.) *Duality and unity of the brain: Unified functioning and specialization of the hemispheres.* London: Macmillan Press Ltd, 1987.

Hirst, W. 'Improving Memory.' In M. Gazzaniga (ed.) *Perspectives in memory research.* Cambridge, Mass.: The MIT Press, 1988.

Hooper, J., and Teresi, D. *The Three-pound Universe.* New York: Dell Publishing Co. Inc., 1986.

Howe, M.J.A. 'Using Students' Notes to Examine the Role of the Individual Learner in Acquiring Meaningful Subject Matter.' *Journal of Educational Research* 64, 61–3.

Hunt, E., and Love, T. 'How Good Can Memory Be?' In A.W. Melton and E. Martin (eds) *Coding Processes in Human Memory*, Washington, DC: Winston,Wiley, 1972, op.

Hunter, I.M.L. 'An Exceptional Memory.' *British Journal of Psychology* 68, 155–64, 1977.

Kandel, E.R., and Schwartz, J.H. 'Molecular biology of learning: Modulation of transmitter release.' *Science* 218, 433–43, 1982.

Keyes, Daniel. *The Minds of Billy Milligan.* New York: Random House,1981; London: Bantam, 1982.

Kimble, D.P. *Biological Psychology.* New York: Holt, Rinehart and Winston Inc., 1988.

Kinsbourne, M., and **Cook, J.** 'Generalized and lateralized effects of concurrent verbalization on a unimanual skill.' *Quarterly Journal of Experimental Psychology* **23**, 341–5, 1971.

Korn, E.R. 'The use of altered states of consciousness and imagery in physical and pain rehabilitation.' *Journal of Mental Imagery* **7** (1), 25–34, 1983.

Kosslyn, S.M. *Ghosts in the Mind's Machine.* New York: W.W. Norton & Co., 1983.

Kosslyn, S.M. 'Imagery in Learning.' In M. Gazzaniga (ed.) *Perspectives in Memory Research.* Cambridge, Mass.: The MIT Press, 1988.

Kosslyn, S.M., Ball, R.M., and **Reiser, B.J.** 'Visual images preserve metric spatial information: Evidence from studies of image scanning.' *Journal of Experimental Psychology: Human Perception and Performance* **4**, 47–60, 1978.

Kotulak, Ronald. *Inside the Brain.* Andrews McMeel Publishing, 1997.

LaBerge, S. *Lucid Dreaming.* New York: Ballantine Books, 1985.

LaPorte, R.E., and **Nath, R.** 'Role of performance goals in prose learning.' *Journal of Educational Psychology* **68**, 260–4, 1976.

Leeds, R., Wedner, E., and **Bloch, B.** *What to say when: A guide to more effective communication.* Dubuque, Iowa: Wm. C. Brown Co. Publishers, 1988.

Loftus, E.F. *Eyewitness Testimony.* Cambridge, Mass.: Harvard University Press, 1980.

Loftus, E.F., and **Zanni, G.** 'Eyewitness testimony: The influence of wording of a question.' *Bulletin of the Psychonomic Society* **5**, 86–8, 1975.

Luria, A.R. *The Mind of a Mnemonist.* London: Jonathan Cape, 1969.

Madigan, S.A. 'Interserial repetition and coding processes in free recall.' *Journal of Verbal Learning and Verbal Behavior* **8**, 828–35, 1969.

Matlin, W.M. *Cognition.* New York: Holt, Rinehart & Winston Inc., 1989.

Mayer, R.E. *Thinking, problem solving, cognition.* New York: W.H. Freeman & Co., 1983.

Mendak, P.A. 'Reading and the Art of Guessing.' *Reading World* **22** (4), 346–51, May 1983.

Miller, G.A. 'The magical number seven, plus or minus two: Some limits on our capacity for processing information.' *Psychological Review* **63**, 81–97, 1956.

Miller, W.H. *Reading Diagnosis Kit.* West Nyack, NY: The Centre for Applied Research in Education, 1978.

Neisser, U. *Memory Observed: Remembering in Natural Contexts.* San Francisco: W.H. Freeman & Co., 1982.

Nelson, T.O. 'Savings and forgetting from long-term memory.' *Journal of Verbal Learning and Verbal Behavior* **10**, 568–76, 1971.

Ornstein, R. *The Psychology of Consciousness.* New York: Harcourt Brace Jovanovich, 1977.

Paivio, A. 'Effects of imagery instructions and concreteness of memory pegs in a mnemonic system,' *Proceedings of the 76th Annual Convention of the American Psychological Association*, 77–8, 1968.

Paivio, A. *Imagery and Verbal Processes.* New York: Holt, Rinehart & Winston Inc., 1971.

Penfield, W., and Perot, P. 'The Brain's Record of Auditory and Visual Experience: A Final Summary and Discussion.' *Brain* **86**, 595–702.

Penfield, W., and Roberts, L. *Speech and Brain-Mechanisms.* Princeton, NJ: Princeton University Press, 1959.

Penry, J. *Looking at Faces and Remembering Them: A Guide to Facial Identification.* London: Elek Books, 1971, op.

Recht, D.R. and Leslie, L. 'Effect of prior knowledge on good and poor readers' memory of text.' *Journal of Educational Psychology* **80** (1), 16–20, 1988.

Reid, G. 'Accelerated learning: Technical training can be fun.' *Training and Development Journal* **39** (9), 24–7, 1985.

Reystak, R.M. *The Mind.* Toronto: Bantam Books, 1988.

Rickards, J.P., and DiVesta, F.J. 'Type and frequency of questions of processing textual materials.' *Journal of Educational Psychology* **66** (3), 354–62, 1974.

Robertson-Tchabo, E.A., Hausman, C.P., and Arenberg, D. 'A classical mnemonic for older learners: A trip that works!' In K.W. Schaie and J. Geiwitz (eds) *Adult development and aging.* Boston: Little, Brown & Co, 1982.

Robinson, A.D. 'What you see is what you get.' *Training and Development Journal* **38** (5), 34–9, 1984.

Rogers, T.B., Kuiper, N.A., and Kirker, W.S. 'Self-reference and the encoding of personal information.' *Journal of Personality and Social Psychology* **35**, 677–88, 1977.

Rosenfield, I. *The Invention of Memory: A New View of the Brain*. New York: Basic Books Inc., 1988.

Rossi, E.L. *The Psychobiology of Mind–Body Healing: New Concepts of Therapeutic Hypnosis*. New York: W.W. Norton & Co., 1986.

Ruger, H.A., and Bussenius, C.E. *Memory*. New York: Teachers College Press, 1913, op.

Russell, Peter. *The Brain Book*. London: Routledge & Kegan Paul, 1966; Ark, 1984.

Schachter, S., and Singer, J.E. 'Cognitive, social and physiological determinants of emotional state.' *Psychological Review* **69**, 377–99, 1962.

Schaie, K.W., and Geiwitz, J. *Adult Development and Aging*. Boston: Little, Brown & Co., 1982.

Siegel, B.S. *Love, Medicine and Miracles*. New York: Harper & Row, 1986.

Skinner, B.F. *The Behavior of Organisms; An Experimental Analysis*. New York: Appleton-Century-Crofts, 1938.

Snyder, S.H. *Drugs and the Brain*. New York: W.H. Freeman & Co., 1986.

Sperling, G.A. 'The information available in brief visual presentation.' *Psychological Monographs* **74**, Whole No. 498, 1960.

Sperry, R.W. 'Hemispheric deconnection and unity in conscious awareness.' *Scientific American* **23**, 723–33, 1968.

Springer, S., and Deutch, G. *Left Brain, Right Brain*. New York: W.H. Freeman & Co., 1985.

Standing, Lionel. 'Learning 10,000 Pictures.' *Quarterly Journal of Experimental Psychology* **25**, 207–22, 1973.

Stratton, George M. 'The Mnemonic Feat of the 'Shass Pollak'.' *Physiological Review* **24**, 244–7, 1917.

Suzuki, S. *Nurtured by love: a new approach to education*. New York: Exposition Press, 1969.

Tart, C.T. *Altered States of Consciousness*. New York: John Wiley & Sons Inc. 1969.

Thomas, E.J. 'The Variation of Memory with Time for Information Appearing During a Lecture.' *Studies in Adult Education,* 57–62, April 1972.

Toffler, A. *Power Shift: knowledge, wealth and violence in the twenty first century*. London: Bantam Books, 1992.

Tulving, E. 'The Effects of Presentation and Recall of Materials in Free-Recall Learning.' *Journal of Verbal Learning and Verbal Behaviour* **6**, 175–84, 1967.

Van Wagenen, W., and Herren, R. 'Surgical division of commissural pathways in the corpus callosum.' *Archives of Neurology and Psychiatry* **44**, 740–59, 1940.

von Restorff, H. 'Über die Wirkung von Bereichsbildungen im Spurenfeld.' *Psychologische Forschung* **18**, 299–342, 1933.

Wagner, D. 'Memories of Morocco: the influence of age, schooling and environment on memory.' *Cognitive Psychology* **10**, 1–28, 1978.

Walsh, D.A. 'Age difference in learning and memory.' In D.S. Woodruff and J.E. Birren (eds) *Aging: Scientific perspectives and Social Issues*. Monterey, Cal: Brooks/Cole Publishing Co., 1975.

Warren, R.M., and Warren, R.P. 'Auditory illusions and confusions.' *Scientific American* **223**, 30–6, 1970.

Winston, Robert. *The Human Mind and How to Make the Most of it*. London: Transworld/BBC, 2003.

Wolford, G. 'Function of distinct associations for paired-associate performance.' *Psychological Review* **73**, 303–13, 1971.

Yates, F.A. *The Art of Memory*. London: Routledge & Kegan Paul, 1966; Ark, 1984.

Zaidel, E. 'A response to Gazzaniga: Language in the right hemisphere: Convergent perspectives.' *American Psychologist* **38** (5), 542–6, 1983.

Index

Unleash the power of your mind with these bestselling titles from the world's leading authority on the brain and learning...

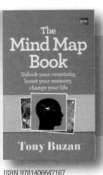

The original and the best book on Mind Maps from their world-renowned inventor.

ISBN 9781406647167

Unlock the power of your brain to transform your business practice and performance with the ultimate 21st Century business tool – the Mind Map.

ISBN 9781406642902

Revolutionise the way you read with the ultimate guide to reading, understanding and learning at amazing speeds.

ISBN 9781406644296

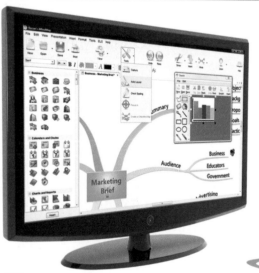